Joanna Blythman is Britain's leading investigative food journalist and an influential commentator on the British food chain. She has won three prestigious awards for her writing, including a Glenfiddich Special Award for her first book, *The Food We Eat*, in 1997, a Caroline Walker Media Award for 'Improving the Nation's Health by Means of Good Food', and a Guild of Food Writers Award in 1997, also for *The Food We Eat*. In 1999 Fourth Estate publish *The Food Our Children Eat*. Joanna Blythman writes for the *Guardian*, several other magazines and newspapers, and broadcasts frequently on food issues.

In her writing and broadcasting, Joanna Blythman has campaigned consistently against genetic modification of food since 1992, airing the issues in a wide range of newspapers, magazines, and on TV and radio. She devoted a chapter to it in her seminal book *The Food We Eat*. In partnership with Greenpeace, she launched 'Food Writers against Gene Foods' at the Savoy in London in January 1999. At this unprecedented event, 150 of the UK's leading

How to Avoid GM Food

Also by Joanna Blythman

The Food We Eat
The Food Our Children Eat

How to Avoid GM Food

Hundreds of brands, products
and ingredients to avoid

Joanna Blythman

FOURTH ESTATE • LONDON

First published in Great Britain in 1999 by
Fourth Estate Limited
6 Salem Road
London W2 4BU

10 9 8 7 6 5 4 3 2 1

A catalogue record for this book is available from the
British Library.

ISBN 1-84115-187-4

Typeset in Adobe Concorde by
Rowland Phototypesetting Ltd, Bury St Edmunds, Suffolk
Printed in Great Britain by Clays Ltd, St Ives plc

For my husband, Nick, who lived and breathed GM along with me

Author's note

Every effort has been made to see that the information in this book is reliable and correct before going to press. However, the whole area of GM food is an extremely fluid one, peppered with grey areas open to differing interpretations. The author has attempted to do justice to this complicated and ever-changing subject, but inevitably some changes in company and regulatory policy will occur after publication.

Acknowledgements

The author would like to thank the following individuals and organisations who generously provided information and support in the writing of this book: Frances Allen, Lynda Brown, Matthew Fort, Lindsay Keenan, Eric Millstone, Rose Pipes, Craig Sams, Julie Sheppard, Peter Stevenson, Lizzie Vann, Friends of the Earth, Genetix Alert, Genewatch, Greenpeace, Women's Environmental Network, Women's Nutritional Advisory Service.

Contents

Part 4 Directory of supermarket foods with GM labels

A few pages to read first

British consumers have undergone a rude awakening on the issue of genetically modified foods. Poll after poll shows that between 70 and 90 per cent of us do not want to eat GM foods and would even support a ban or at least a freeze on their sale – yet despite that, we've got them anyway.

Genetically modified ingredients are now turning up, mainly unlabelled, in everyday foods we take for granted – from baby food and pizza through to sandwiches and ready meals. The realisation that genetically modified foods have been effectively foisted on us, without our consent, has left many people feeling angry, frustrated and powerless. And when government jumps to the tune of the transnational biotech companies who hope to profit from this new untested technology, undemocratically ignoring the will of the people, we are entitled to feel this way. A sense of powerlessness creeps in. The widespread presence of genetically modified ingredients can seem like a *fait accompli*: why fight the inevitable?

But such fatalism is not justified. The post-BSE British public has had a rapid crash course on food issues. We are fed up with technological tinkering with our precious food chain, driven by corporate greed. What we want is more safe, naturally produced and organic food, food grown with respect for the environment that does not compromise human health or turn farm animals into industrial machines.

We are no longer a naïve and easily baffled nation when it comes to consumer issues. The phrases 'best scientific advice', 'no proof of risk' and the like simply provoke a hollow laugh. Exaggerated claims that new technologies are going to save the world from hunger and give us ever more perfect food fall on increasingly deaf ears: we heard this all before with pesticides and factory-farming and we know where it got us. Post BSE, any illusion that we can trust government to protect the environment and human health has gone by the board. Revelations about the extent to which our Government is in bed with the biotech industry just underline what we already suspected. Our would-be protectors cannot be relied upon to fight for consumers on this one. They are too busy creating a 'supportive climate' in the UK for the biotech industry.

With this heightened awareness, the British public – once galvanised into action – is a frightening opponent, one which even the global might of the biotech industry has cause to fear. By putting our foot down here and systematically boycotting products and companies who are bringing genetically modified food to our tables, we can be tremendously effective. Action of this kind in the UK strengthens the long-established opposition throughout Europe, opposition that is already strong and vocal in Germany, France and Switzerland.

When a European public refuses to have genetically modified foods slipped compliantly down its throat, the reverberations will be felt in North America, where genetic engineers have pulled off the feat of getting GM foods on to the shelves without any labelling. They have managed this because they have undue influence with the regulators and systematically squash any opposition to their products with heavy-handed threats of legal action. The North American consumer has not lived through BSE and tends to believe that government can be trusted to safeguard public health and the environment. It is a great sleeping giant, still amazingly unaware of the genetic manipulation of its foods. A more aware European public is already helping it to wake up.

So this book tells you how to use the power of your shopping basket – in a creative and effective way – against genetically modified food. First of all, it enables you to shop defensively. It arms you with general strategies for eliminating genetically modified food from your diet, both when you shop and when you eat out. It maps out the zones of most contaminated food and identifies key ingredients which may be genetically modified. In the Directory, you'll find a detailed list of genetically modified food products you can boycott specifically.

Next, this book enables you to shop positively, because it steers you in the direction of brands, companies and retailers that have adopted an anti-genetic modification position. You can give them your business and support and encourage others to follow suit.

If you use this book to boycott GM food, you will be sending a powerful message to food producers, manufacturers and retailers that as far as the British public is concerned, genetically modified foods are commercial death. Such action is already producing results. Because of public opposition, many large food manu-facturers and retailers who might otherwise have embraced genetically modified ingredients unquestioningly are now becoming distinctly twitchy. They do not want to see their meticulously tended brand images tarnished by association with a new, inadequately tested and potentially catastrophic technology. Why should they become doormats for the biotech companies if they only disenchant their cus-tomers in the process? Many are wondering which way to jump. Armed with this book, you can use your shopping basket to concentrate their minds.

It is written in a partisan way and makes absolutely no attempt to outline the arguments offered in favour of GM food. No apology is forthcoming. The British public has heard the propaganda onslaught from the biotech com-panies and noted their disingenuous efforts to claim that all science is on their side. The pro-GM food lobby has been working away on reg-ulators for over a decade in the hope that a behind-the-scenes carve-up would get round the need for any public debate. This lobby has tried to soft-soap the British public with patronisingly simplistic and spurious arguments designed to obfuscate its true motivation: corporate greed. When this failed, it retreated into characterising any opposition to its expansionist plans as superstitious and unscientific hysteria – despite the fact that many eminent scientists are opposed to GM food and are campaigning against it. Fortunately, the pro-GM food lobby got caught out and most of us have heard enough from it for the time being.

While this battle for control of our food chain rages, it is important that British consumers send out a simple message that anyone can understand. Call these food ingredients genetically modified, genetically engineered, GE, GM, or GMO if you like. Either way, we've firmly said that we do not want to eat them. Please use this book to underscore that message.

Part 1

Why you might not want to eat genetically modified food

Genetic modification is quite different from traditional ways of improving food

Proponents of genetic modification say that genetic modification will give us better and more nutritious food, reduce our use of pesticides and save the world from hunger – without any downside whatsoever. They present new genetically manipulated foods as an unthreatening extension of long-accepted selective breeding techniques which have already improved our food. In the past farmers bred, for example, their best strains of wheat to produce preferred hybrid strains, or different types of cattle to develop new breeds with certain sought-after characteristics – such as the celebrated Aberdeen Angus.

However, such selective breeding never went beyond the limits of what might occur in nature through cross-pollination, hybridisation and mating. It was only carried out within established species barriers: corn with corn, pigs with pigs and so on. Any changes or improvements that were produced by this type of breeding were slow and in keeping with what might have occurred naturally in any case, over time.

Species that were closely related but not identical – such as the horse and the donkey – were able to interbreed, but their offspring were usually infertile, like the horse/donkey cross: the mule. Breeders viewed this as a natural safety device, to prevent the mixing of incompatible genes that could produce a genetic accident, such as malformations and hereditary weaknesses, and also to ensure the survival of each species.

Modern genetic modification – basically a test tube science developed since the seventies and still in its infancy – is substantially different from this very slow and canny selective breeding in two major respects. First, it produces instant changes and not the slow, tried and tested, evolving change of traditional breeding. Second, it differs radically from the circumspect 'like with like' traditional approach because it allows genes from distinct and totally diverse species to be swapped around and used in new combinations that could never occur in nature. Here are some examples:

- A gene from a soil bacterium has been inserted into soy beans to make them resistant to a particular herbicide

- A gene from an Arctic fish has been inserted into tomatoes to make them frost-resistant.

In the future, if genetic modification progresses unchecked, our food could consist of a series of new food 'constructions', assembled from genes taken from thousands of unrelated plants, animals, insects, viruses and bacteria.

Even where modern genetic-modification techniques are being applied within species barriers and between similar crops or animals, they can be used to bring about instant changes which would have taken years to happen in nature.

So genetic modification of food in its modern form is fundamentally different from traditional selective breeding, both in terms of the limits of the breeding and the pace at which changes can occur.

Modern genetic modification is imprecise and unpredictable

Modern genetic-modification techniques allow scientists to isolate and identify a gene which produces a desired characteristic, copy it, then insert (splice) it into another species. In theory, it is the ultimate in designer food, where scientists can alter crops to be ever more perfect and adapted to our needs.

But even though it is possible to change food in this way, genetic engineers still have an inadequate understanding of how genes work, not only in isolation, but also in combination with one another. The complexity of the interrelationships between genes within a group, let alone genes from different groups, is only just beginning to be appreciated.

This means that modern genetic modification is still inherently an imprecise and unpredictable technology. Its proponents like to make out that it is as carefully honed and sophisticated a technique as keyhole surgery. The reality, however, is that it is more like a blunderbuss. It consists of the crude cutting and splicing of genes based on experiments as to how a gene behaves in a test tube. This does not tell us how that gene operates in its natural context or how it might behave when inserted into another species. So even the most brilliant molecular biologists can only hazard a guess at the ramifications such cut-and-paste changes could have throughout the food chain. With such an incomplete understanding, many people want a more cautious approach to be adopted. But genetic modification techniques are being applied to food production on a wide scale, and at breakneck speed.

The risks are huge and the effects irreversible

In the second half of the twentieth century, we have begun to see the catastrophic effects that some technological 'progress' has had on human health and the environment. The routine use of synthetic chemical pesticides has put paid to much of our native wildlife and poisoned our food and water. The unnatural practice of feeding recycled animal protein to herbivores to make them more productive gave us BSE and its human equivalent, new variant CJD. This disease has already claimed human lives.

But the risks posed by genetically modified foods make the hazards of pesticides and BSE pale by comparison. Unlike dangerous car seats or exploding fireworks, there is no product recall for altered genes once they are released into the environment. In theory, it is possible to clean up pesticide pollution in time. If we are very lucky, and extremely careful, we may be able to eliminate BSE and new variant CJD eventually. This damage can be undone. But once the mistaken results of genetic manipulations are out there in the environment, they could be passed on to future generations for perpetuity. We cannot predict what knock-on effects they might have, or even know where to look for these effects. There is no simple way of reining them in or containing them.

Nature is a beautifully organised and complex system which we do not fully understand. When we allow even the brightest scientists to start tinkering around with genes – the very building blocks of life – we are likely unwittingly to trigger some unintended and irreversible side-effects.

So far, limited genetic modification experiments have produced some very problematic results:

- Fish geneticists have succeeded in producing a bigger and faster-growing 'super salmon', but it also turned out to be deformed

- The soy bean which was given a brazil-nut gene to boost its protein level transferred the brazil-nut allergen to the soy bean. People who were sensitive to brazil nuts and ate the bean developed allergic reactions to it.

Mishaps like this have not so far got on to the market because their faults were easily spotted. However, complex changes triggered by genetic manipulation could take time to show up and turn up in places in the environment – or affect other organisms – which had not been considered. There might be no way of halting or containing the unintended effects caused, once discovered.

Genetically modified food could seriously mess up the environment

Genetic pollution and superweeds

The biggest worry is that genetically modified crops cannot be contained effectively once released into the environment. Birds will be birds and bees will be bees. Pollen can travel surprisingly long distances, either carried by bees or blown on the wind. Researchers have shown this to be anything from 2.5 to 9 kilometres. Even with a perimeter 'cordon sanitaire' around fields sowed with genetically modified crops, they could cross-pollinate or hybridise with other crops and weeds, and accidentally transfer their altered characteristics to them. The effects could be ruinous. One study has indicated that genetically modified oil seed rape can breed with other related crops and render them inedible.

Genes inserted into a crop could also give it a competitive advantage over existing conventional crops. A new genetically modified variety could effectively turn into an escaped weed which dominates the environment, a usurping pest which displaces more traditional crops and the wildlife which depends on them.

There is also the alarming prospect of 'superweeds'. It has already been demonstrated that genes from oil seed rape, genetically modified to be resistant to a certain herbicide, can spread to weeds in the same family. These weeds then become resistant to the same herbicide. Such unintended genetic pollution or spread is impossible to predict and difficult – perhaps impossible – to eradicate.

More pesticides, not less

Despite the biotech industry's initial claims that genetic modification would be the technology that would liberate the world from pesticides, the lion's share of genetically modified crops already on the market, or in the pipeline, have been modified to be used alongside pesticides, not instead of them. For example, Monsanto's Roundup Ready soya bean has been manipulated so that it must be used with the same company's herbicide, 'Roundup Ready'. And just to make sure of this, growers planting this soya have to sign contracts which say that they will only use the company's herbicide.

Until recently, use of pesticides has been restricted by the fact that they might kill both the crop and the targeted weed. Genetically modified crops with inbuilt herbicide resistance make it possible to spray everything that grows in a field. So many environmentalists believe that as more genetically modified crops are grown, our use of pesticides will increase, not decrease.

Diminishing flora and fauna

Many naturalists and wildlife bodies think that the introduction of genetically modified crops will lead to a further intensification of agriculture. More land would be planted with a limited number of genetically modified hybrid crop 'monocultures' and there would be less need for traditional crop rotations where land is rested and the same crop is not grown in the same place for years at a time. Such intensification, in combination with increased pesticide usage, could speed up the already alarming decline in habitat diversity in the UK, putting the future existence of many beneficial wildlife species under threat. Species already identified as being particularly vulnerable include bats, skylarks, song thrushes, newts and crickets.

Many genetically modified crops have been manipulated to be resistant or tolerant to pesticides or to have an inbuilt disease or insect resistance. It is possible that they could pass these traits on to non-beneficial insects and pests which would then be much more difficult to control. It is also possible that they could effectively become toxic to beneficial wildlife such as ladybirds and bees.

Genetically modified food could adversely affect human health

Many scientists are concerned that once foreign genes are inserted into a food, they disturb the chemical functioning of that food. This could produce unforeseen health risks in the form of

new allergens and toxins, and other unpredictable health effects. There is already some
research which indicates how serious these
problems could be. For example:

• One study has indicated that genes inserted
  into crops to give them antibiotic resistance
  can be passed to bacteria in the gut. The
  worry is that the efficacy of antibiotics in
  human (and animal) health could be
  seriously compromised as farm animals and
  humans consume foods containing antibiotic-resistance marker genes, inadvertently
  creating antibiotic-resistant 'superbugs'

Potential health risks from GM food could span
everything from an instant and specific adverse
reaction (i.e. an allergic reaction triggered in
the individual who consumes the food) to a
gradual, cumulative effect in people who consume genetically modified foods over time, or
even a knock-on effect for people who have not
eaten the food. An antibiotic-resistant superbug
caused by the inclusion of antibiotic-resistance
genes in food could seriously affect people who
have never eaten any genetically modified food
at all. Once they became ill with a certain infec-
tion, the antibiotics normally used to deal with
it could already have been rendered ineffective.

Genetically modified foods are being tested inadequately and marketed prematurely

All-embracing reassurances that new genetically modified foods are safe and rigorously tested flow from the mouths of regulators and government ministers. Consumers are told that new foods with altered genes can only be allowed on to the market once they have passed through strict testing procedures to establish that they are safe. Unfortunately, the reality of testing does not support those assurances.

Sweeping assumptions have been made

The regulatory principle underlying testing of genetically modified foods is the notion of 'substantial equivalence'. The biotech companies pushing genetically modified foods lobbied heavily for this principle, which assumes that new genetically modified foods operate in a similar manner to their conventional lookalikes. So the relevant regulatory bodies assume that if a genetically modified food is chemically the same as the conventionally produced variety, there need be no concerns about its safety.

Testing of safety is very limited and narrow

The 'substantial equivalence' principle means that safety testing is restricted to a fairly straightforward set of chemical comparisons. For example, are vitamin C levels similar? Are the crop's processing characteristics the same? Is the fatty-acid profile of the food the same? If the answers to such questions are 'yes', then a new food is likely to get the go-ahead. Unfortunately, chemical differences in genetically modified foods may be very small and not identified by existing tests. For example, the adverse effects of eating BSE-infected beef would not have been picked up by this limited type of analysis.

Regulatory committees do look at potential health risks such as whether or not known allergens or toxins are being transferred. But they do not consider any unknown or new problems that might be caused. Since even the most minute chemical alteration of a food can trigger an unintended reaction, they do not even know where to look for that reaction.

Field trials are not food trials

When government ministers refer to 'rigorous safety assessment' of genetically modified foods, this sounds much more reassuring than it really is. They are referring to the limited chemical testing described above, carried out in a laboratory, followed by greenhouse tests and then open-field trials. The truth is that the only way to test the safety of these foods is for people to eat them over a reasonable length of time. No such food trials have been conducted before these crops have come to market. When we eat them, we consumers are actually testing these new foods for the first time. Once we are eating them along with other conventional foods, any adverse health affects will be hard, even impossible, to monitor.

Unlike new drugs which have to go through years of trials, first on animals, then on human volunteers, genetically altered foods can whizz through the regulatory hoops in record time with nothing like the testing required for drugs. But if a genetically modified food did turn out to have adverse affects, it would have the capacity to produce irreversible adverse health effects which could affect many more people than any drug, without any therapeutic benefits to offset them.

Wider implications for the environment are not addressed

The effects of introducing genetically modified crops into the environment are only considered by regulatory committees in a very restricted way. Genetically modified crops are given the go-ahead on the basis of laboratory tests, greenhouse trials and then very small-scale, experimental field trials. This testing does not show how the crops might actually behave when grown on a large scale in diverse natural environments and the analysis of results observed concentrates on providing information mainly on economic characteristics such as yield.

Potential environmental risks of genetically modified crops are considered on an individual, crop-by-crop basis, not alongside any other genetically modified crops which might also be approved. This means that the cumulative impact of several such crops growing together in the environment is not addressed.

The secondary consequences of the introduction of genetically modified crops into the environment are also left untested. What impact might this crop have on wildlife? Will it affect crop diversity? Will it mean that more pesticides are used? Will it prejudice other more natural farming systems? For example, might organic farmers' crops be contaminated by gene flow from genetically modified crops in the vicinity? Such broader questions are not addressed.

Genetic modification could increase animal suffering

Intensification of factory farming

Conventional selective breeding techniques have concentrated on speeding up the length of time it takes for an animal to reach maturity, and increasing the amount of meat it will finally produce. Even in conventional breeding, farm animals are very often pushed beyond their metabolic and physiological limits, increasing their suffering and undermining their health.

Cases in point include:

- Turkeys bred to have such large breasts that they can no longer mate naturally and have to be artificially inseminated using invasive and unnatural techniques

- The cattle variety (called Belgian Blue) overbred to such an extent that often the females can no longer calve naturally

- 'Supersows' bred to have eighteen instead of twelve teats and ever larger litters, however exhausting that might be

- Broiler chickens bred to grow faster, but whose leg muscles and bones cannot support the rapid growth.

Both the research goals driving modern genetic modification in the field of animal production to date and the practical applications to which it has been put suggest that genetic modification will be used to crank up even further the extent to which farm animals are pushed beyond their natural limits in the name of more 'efficient' production.

One example of this is the genetically modified growth hormone, recombinant bovine somatotropin (rBST). This is a genetically modified copy of the hormone that cows produce naturally which stimulates milk production. However, some scientists think it produces adverse affects in cows. The Canadian Government, for example, has not licensed the hormone for sale because it concluded that it increases the frequency of udder infections by 25 per cent and lameness by 50 per cent.

Laboratories on legs

There are concerns that animals are already viewed by the biotechnology industry as prime candidates for genetic experimentation and as 'laboratories on legs' – treasure troves of genes that can be raided for experimental purposes. Although the total number of experiments on animals is falling overall, the use of animals for genetic-modification experiments is actually increasing. It is felt that in the drive to find genes which can be introduced into foodstuffs, or in the rush to make them more 'productive', animals will be subjected to more experimentation and their unnecessary suffering correspondingly increased.

One unfortunate example of this was the 'Beltsville pigs'. In the 1980s, in the US, these pigs were given genes from both humans and cattle in an attempt to make them put on more lean meat faster. This genetic experiment turned into an infamous animal health disaster and had to be abandoned because the pigs developed damaged vision, deformed skulls and were unable to walk properly.

Animal genes in vegetarian food

Although there are no genetically modified foods containing animal genes on the market yet, many experiments along these lines have been carried out. In the future, we could be in a situation where vegetarian foods – such as tomatoes, potatoes or flour – contained an animal gene. Obviously this is unacceptable to vegetarians and religions that proscribe the eating of certain types of meat. GM foods with animal genes would need to be labelled under existing regulations. However, as foods come on to the market which contain genes from many diverse sources, it could become increasingly hard to keep track of what genetic manipulations had been made. 'Vegetarian' products with animal genes could become difficult to identify and avoid.

Genetic modification of food is driven by private profit, not public interest

Genetically modified foods have not appeared on our shelves in response to consumer demand. In fact, the opposite is the case: an overwhelming number of people throughout the UK and Europe have indicated that they do not want to eat such food.

However, genetically modified foods have been forced on to the market, and rushed through an inadequate regulatory framework, by large, profit-driven transnational corporations. These are the same corporations that brought us drugs to be used as props in the intensive factory-farming of animals, drugs that allow livestock to be kept in unhealthy and unnatural circumstances yet produce meat and milk in ever greater quantities.

They are also the same corporations that gave us 'The Green Revolution' of pesticides and hybrid crops, which they presented as the 'solution' to world hunger. This exaggerated claim has been widely discredited as large sections of the world's population continue to go hungry while widespread use of pesticides and modern hybrid crops have had a disastrous effect on biodiversity (the range and biological diversity of crops in production). Now these corporations are touting genetic modification as the technology that is going to feed the world, making even more exaggerated claims that it will improve food to suit our needs and liberate us from the very same pesticides that they designed.

Any illusion that genetic modification of food will be used benevolently and in the public good is given the lie by the nature of genetically modified foods now on our shelves and in the pipeline. The vast majority of these crops are designed to be used along with pesticides, not instead of them. Other changes in the traits of food – such as modification of tomatoes to last longer without rotting – seem to deliver benefits only to processors, not consumers. In Third World countries, genetically modified crops are widely opposed. It seems that the people we are told such crops are meant to help are not persuaded of their benefits either.

Genetic modification of food allows a few powerful corporations to control the food chain

Throughout the world, there is mounting concern that genetic modification of food will be used to allow powerful corporations to effectively privatise the food chain by owning and controlling food production. These corporations are already involved in patenting food crops, using the fact that they have genetically modified them as a basis for that ownership. Gradually they are taking what was everyone's free biological heritage and claiming it as their own.

In tandem with this, they are charging farmers for their 'improved' seeds and building into them 'Terminator' genes, which means that the seeds are only good for one year and cannot be saved for the next harvest. This ensures that farmers have to pay for them each year. And by buying up small, independent seed companies which might still sell conventional, unaltered fertile seed, they could leave farmers with no other option but to do business with them.

Some 80 per cent of all patents on genetically modified crops are currently held by only thirteen transnational corporations. This underlines how genetic modification of food is being used as a mechanism by which a handful of powerful companies attempt to control the food chain.

Genetic modification of food threatens the existence of organic farming

At present, people can buy organic food if they are concerned about food quality and the effect conventional farming has had on the environment. The strict rules which govern organic farming do not allow genetic modification of crops or animals. However, once genetically modified crops are being grown widely, it will be impossible for organic farmers to prevent their crops being contaminated with gene flow from such crops, for the reasons explained above. This would mean that they could no longer guarantee that their food was strictly organic.

The growth of genetically modified crops threatens the very existence of organic farming and deprives consumers of choice. Once genetically modified crops are in production in a major way, there would be no true organic alternative.

It is clear that, at present, consumer demand for organic food is already outstripping supply. Once genetically modified crops are the order of the day, consumers will suffer a double blow. There will be more food that we do not want around (genetically modified) and less or no availability of the food we do want (organic).

There's nothing to be lost by holding back

Irrespective about how you feel about the issues raised above, there is one very sensible and cool reason for avoiding genetically modified food: there is nothing to be lost by holding back. This is why many organisations are calling for a ban, moratorium or freeze on their current development. The promises dangled before our eyes by corporations pushing genetically modified food are not one-off, chance-of-a-lifetime deals. If they are so great, and they have no downside, as is being claimed, then we can look forward to them in the future when they have undergone much more stringent testing, passed through tighter regulatory hoops with flying colours and arrived on our plates in a slow, careful and measured way.

At the moment, however, genetically modified foods are being introduced on to the market with indecent haste. They represent the first products of a new, risky and crude technology that has been inadequately tested. If it goes wrong, it will make the fall-out from BSE seem like child's play. Genetically modified ingredients are turning up in our food against our wishes and, in the main, without our knowledge. This makes them a proposition that many thinking consumers may wish to avoid.

Part 2

Why you can't rely on labels

The labelling regulations are restricted and full of loopholes

The labelling regulations which cover new genetically modified foods were put together hastily and under pressure from large biotechnology companies who wanted to get their products into the general food supply quickly. By the time genetically modified soya and maize were entering the food chain in 1998, there was no labelling system up and running. So they were actually introduced initially without any legal requirement to label.

Two waves of belated labelling rules have since been put in place. However, these reflect the intense lobbying brought to bear on European regulators by the biotech companies who are developing genetically modified foods. They have argued consistently against the labelling of such foods on the grounds that it would discourage consumers from buying their products and have been successful in the US in seeing that genetically modified foods do not need to carry labels.

In Europe, however, these companies have had to give in to demands for informative labelling, but have been working away behind the scenes to ensure that although they might sound adequate, labelling requirements are in fact as generous to them as possible.

They have succeeded in underpinning all labelling with the 'substantial equivalence' principle. This assumes that, in the main, genetically modified food ingredients operate in the same way as conventional ones, and therefore there is no need to differentiate the two categories by a label. So, in effect, once the regulatory labelling criteria as now drawn up are applied, only a small number of those foods that contain a genetically modified ingredient need to be labelled.

The labelling regulations also assume that consumers aren't interested in how a food was produced, just what is in the end product. So foods which have been genetically modified at some point in their production do not need to be labelled at all, unless protein or DNA from a GM crop can be detected in the food after it has been processed.

Only a few foods need to be labelled, most don't

Labelled foods

The only genetically modified foods that need to be labelled are:

- Those that contain detectable DNA or protein from a genetically modified crop

- Those whose composition, nutritional value or intended use is different from conventional foods (such as a potato which has been modified to change the amount of starch it contains)

- Those that raise ethical issues, such as animal genes in foods eaten by vegetarians

- Those which could give rise to allergic reactions (such as a peanut gene inserted into a non-nut food).

Unlabelled foods

None of these genetically modified foods need to be labelled:

- Foods containing a 'derivative' of a GM crop where no DNA or protein from that crop can be detected (such as oil from GM soya or modified starch from GM maize). Such derivatives turn up in between 60 and 80 per cent of processed foods

- Foods containing a GM food additive (such as the emulsifier E322 soya lecithin). The term 'additive' is used to cover all flavourings, preservatives, colours, emulsifiers, acids, acidity regulators, anti-caking agents, anti-foaming agents, antioxidants, firming agents, flavour enhancers, flour treatment agents, foam stabilisers, gelling agents, glazing agents, humectants, modified starches, stabilisers, sweeteners, thickeners and yeast nutrients

- Foods which use genetic-modification processes or methods at some point in their production (such as enzymes in breadmaking or hormones to produce milk)

- Foods containing detectable DNA or protein from a GM crop but at a level that is below a certain '*de minimis*' threshold or tolerance. The regulations do not state what this threshold is. Food manufacturers are interpreting this as permitting DNA or protein levels representing anything between 3 and 10 per cent of the total product.

Voluntary labels

In response to consumer demand, some companies have already labelled a few foods to give more information than is required by law. For example, the Co-op labels vegetarian cheese made from the genetically modified substitute for rennet, chymosin, as such. Safeway and Sainsbury's both label their genetically modified Californian tomato purée, even though the law doesn't demand it.

Recently, the big chains have been considering whether or not to label certain ingredients that are derived from genetically modified crops, such as soya oil, even though they are not legally obliged to do so. This would be a massive task because derivatives of genetically modified crops turn up in literally thousands of foods. So any attempt to label them all – if that goes ahead – will clearly take some time.

To make matters more complicated, different chains apply different criteria as to which derivatives should be labelled, and which should not. This means that from a shopper's point of view, there is no guarantee that a derivative labelled by one chain will necessarily be labelled by another.

In an attempt to make matters clearer to consumers, some brands and retailers opposed to genetic modification of food – notably in the wholefood market – carry labels to that effect. Examples of this include the guarantee 'Contains no genetically modified ingredients' or an asterisk beside a certain ingredient explained below as 'Not genetically modified'. However, such labels are rather inconsistent.

The Vegetarian Society, for example, says that its seal of approval – the vegetarian 'V' symbol – cannot go on products with GM ingredients. But it will allow it to be used to endorse vegetarian cheese made with chymosin, the GM alternative to animal rennet.

Companies can also make a 'non-GM' or 'GM-free' claim as long as their products only contain DNA or protein from a GM crop below the *'de minimis'* threshold limit explained above. Very few companies would knowingly use such claims to mislead. However, many are just not in a position to protect their ingredients from cross-contamination from GM crops. This contamination could occur via cross-pollination, during transport, storage, processing or distribution. Thus, with the best will in the world, even companies or producers making 'GM-free' claims can get caught out. So if you want to avoid genetically modified food, such 'anti'-genetic-modification labels, although presently few and far between, may help cut through the confusion, but they are not a total guarantee.

Labels give a false sense of security

Most consumers want and expect clear-cut, all-embracing labelling of food so that they can tell when genetic-modification manipulations have been carried out. Any comprehensive definition needs to label any food that has been produced using genetic-modification methods at any stage or that contains any major or minor ingredient that has been genetically modified. This is patently not happening since, as outlined above, only a minority of foods which fit that bill need to be labelled by law.

When government ministers reassure consumers not only that genetically modified foods are safe to eat, but also that they are all labelled, they are operating a conveniently limited definition of what constitutes genetic modification of food. This definition is at odds with most people's commonsense understanding and expectations. In other words, when government and consumers talk about labelling, we do not mean the same thing.

Government ministers are also keen to promote the idea that labelling automatically gives consumers the choice as to whether or not they buy genetically modified food. Obviously, when the labelling in operation is so restricted, the promise of choice is not being delivered.

But even if a thorough and totally comprehensive labelling system was put into force, it would not prevent people who assiduously boycotted genetically modified food from being affected by a public health or environmental 'accident' triggered by genetically modified crops or food.

If, for example, the inclusion of antibiotic-resistance genes in foods for both humans and animals does produce the virulent 'superbugs' that some scientists predict, then anyone who gets ill and needs antibiotics could be affected, irrespective of whether they ate those foods. In the scenario where crops genetically modified to be toxic to pests decimate our beneficial wildlife, everyone is affected, whether or not they buy those crops as food.

If you are particularly worried about the effects of chemical food additives, you can cut them out of your diet entirely. If you want to avoid pesticide residues, you can eat organic. But once genetically modified food crops are being produced, no one can opt out of any harmful knock-on effects they might set in motion.

Part 3

How to avoid genetically modified food when you shop

Eat organic food

Eating organic is the most simple single strategy we can adopt if we want to avoid genetically modified food. While the arrival of unsegregated genetically modified crops has left conventional producers and manufacturers floundering in a sea of confusion, the organic movement is crystal clear on the matter. Organic food production totally outlaws genetic modification at any stage. It is regarded as contrary to the spirit of organic farming, which seeks to work with nature, harnessing natural processes to grow wholesome food in demonstrably safe, tried and tested ways.

At a food production level, organic farmers are not allowed to grow genetically modified crops. Nor are they allowed to use genetically modified products such as the growth hormone rBST, which can be injected into cows to make them produce more milk. Any unfortunate organic farmers who find that their farms are too close to fields where genetically modified crops are being grown risk losing their organic certification: tough and unfair though that may be. Strict rules mean that where there is a risk of cross-contamination, organic status will be withdrawn.

When it comes to food processing, organic manufacturers are not allowed to use genetically modified ingredients or processes at all. Both organic food production and manufacturing are subject to regular, independent checks to see that these conditions are being implemented. Unlike their conventional counterparts, organic food producers can give a reliable assurance that their food is 'GM-free' and prove it too.

So, when you eat organic food, you know that it will not be genetically modified. But this is not the only reason to do so. By choosing organic food, you send an important message to the food and farming industry about the kind of food you want to eat.

Many conventional farmers and food producers are sitting on the fence. Should they give in to the great commercial push for genetic technology in our food, should they hold out for conventional supplies, or should they be brave and go organic?

Every time you buy an organic product, you let companies see that there is a good commercial future in traditionally sourced food which is grown and produced naturally. This way, your shopping choices can influence indirectly companies contemplating the pros and cons of going down the genetically modified food path.

Eat unprocessed food

For the time being, there is no whole un-processed genetically-modifed food on our shelves in the UK. There are a few on their way: see 'Genetically modified foods in the pipeline'. But even within the pathetic limitations of the labelling laws now weakly in force, these would have to be labelled and would therefore be easier to spot and avoid than processed deri-vatives. So in the short term, you can limit your exposure to genetically modified food by choos-ing raw, unprocessed food. By contrast, it is thought that between 60 and 90 per cent of all processed foods contain a genetically modified ingredient or use genetic-modification pro-cesses at some point in their production.

However, the term 'processed food' needs to be given some thought. It is common to hear it being applied to downmarket, cheap, conve-nience-type foods (such as Pot Noodles or sauce mixes) and it is easy to think that you do not usually consume these anyway. But as the Directory section in this book shows, many ready-prepared foods with a quite upmarket image do contain genetically modified ingredients. When we pick up a modish-looking ready meal, or a relatively expensive sandwich, we tend not to think of it as a 'processed food' with all the associated negative connotations. And while some people might prefer to bake a potato rather than buy some oven chips, few people make their own cheese or press their own cooking oil. Yet cheese and oil are just two 'processed' products that could well be genetically modified. So before you assume that you are not a processed food consumer, browse through the Directory and the section 'Where you're most likely to find GM food and drinks as you shop'.

Use wholefood shops

Unlike supermarkets, who are wallowing in a sea of confusion over whether or not their foods are genetically modified, the wholefood or 'natural food trade' has taken a proactive attitude to GM food over the last couple of years. Wholefood shops cater especially for vegetarians and therefore stock many products which are soya-based. However, wholefood shoppers, both vegetarian and non-vegetarian, are less likely to welcome genetic modification of food. So the wholefood trade has set about ensuring that it can guarantee that soya and, more recently, maize products are GM-free. It has done this by establishing 'identity-preserved' supplies of non-GM crops. These come with a full pedigree to guarantee that they are what they say they are.

In addition, the wholefood sector has asked companies to sign up to a GM-free declaration, so that consumers can see where familiar companies stand on the matter. So it has built up a 'positive list' of brands that are GM-free. This list is incorporated in the 'green brands' listing in the section 'Where the brands stand on GM food'. Many wholefood shops have a list to consult on the premises.

Wholefood shops these days stock more and more organic foods. All organic foods are guaranteed to be free from genetic modification.

Where you're most likely to find GM food and drinks as you shop

As you navigate your way around a super-market or smaller food shops, it's helpful to know what categories of food are most likely to conceal products that may have been genetically modified so that you can be on your guard. Not all shopping zones are the same in this respect. In certain categories of food – fresh meat, for example – you can afford to be relaxed. While in others – such as sandwiches – extreme vigilance is called for.

You can use the guide below to identify categories or types of food and drink where you need to pay attention.

In the green zone

(You can be sure that, for the time being, none of the foods or drinks in this zone have been genetically modified in any way.)

- Fruit and vegetables, fresh or frozen (*but* watch out for GM whole tomatoes, which are in the pipeline)

- Meat, poultry and game, fresh or frozen, just butchered and cleaned

- Fish and shellfish, fresh or frozen, *but not* processed fish such as fish fingers or processed seafood such as crab sticks

- Eggs in shell

- Coffee (beans, ground and instant)

- Natural teas and herbal infusions without flavourings, either loose or in teabags

- Real cocoa powder

- Milk from the UK or EU (not GM until the end of 1999, but could change thereafter)

- Natural yogurt from the UK or EU (as above)

- Butter from UK or EU milk (as above)

- Soft or curd cheese made from UK or EU milk (as above)

- Unflavoured and uncoated nuts and seeds

- Grains and flour, e.g. wheat, rice, rye, barley, oats

- Dried pasta, egg pasta included

- Dried noodles, plain and egg

- Quorn (in uncooked form)

- Extra virgin olive oil

- Sunflower oil

- Jams, jellies, marmalade and relishes (but only if made with sugar cane or sugar beet)

- Spices, whole or milled

- Herbs, fresh or dried

- Salt

- Vinegar

- Flavourings (natural only)

- Fruit juice

- All spirits and wine.

In the amber zone

(It is possible that foods and drinks in this zone have been genetically modified.)

- Bread and rolls

- Sweet and savoury breads (e.g. croissants, muffins, scones, pikelets)

- Artificial flavourings (e.g. vanilla or peppermint essence)

- Flavoured teas, fruit teas and herbal infusions

- Tinned fruit

- Tinned vegetables

- Tinned fish packed in oil

- Fresh yeast for baking

- Any food fortified with vitamin B2 riboflavin (breakfast cereals, baby food, soft drinks)

- Dried and wet baby food

- Soya formula milk

- Beer.

In the red zone

(It is quite likely that foods and drinks in this zone have been genetically modified.)

- Lo-cal, 'lite' and reduced-fat foods

- Processed foods imported from the US

- Prepared sandwiches

- Prepared ready meals, both meat and vegetarian (especially ethnic-themed ones, e.g. Mexican, Chinese)

- Vegetarian meals containing soya

- Vegetarian products containing soya milk or tofu

- Prepared pasta and noodles

- Processed meat, fish, poultry or vegetarian equivalent, breaded, battered or in crispy crumb

- Cooked sliced meats

- Burgers and meat loaf

- Sausages and sausage rolls

- Pies, pasties, savouries and quiches (both meat and vegetarian)

- Sweet and savoury mousses (such as salmon or chocolate)

- Salad dressings and salsas

- Prepared pizzas

- Hard or semi-hard cheese, cheese spreads

- Sweetened, flavoured yogurts

- Ice-cream, frozen yogurt and non-dairy desserts

- Cooking oil, margarines and spreads

- Mayonnaise
- Ready sauces and stir-fry pastes (such as hoisin or hollandaise)
- Dried fruit
- Crisps and packet snacks (especially flavoured ones)
- Tortilla chips
- Popcorn
- Taco shells
- Biscuits
- Cakes
- Soft drinks and colas
- Hot drinks (such as hot chocolate)
- Chocolate and chocolate confectionery
- Sweets and confectionery
- Tinned and packet soups
- Cake mixes
- Packet sauces (savoury and sweet), trifle and mousse mixes
- Pâtés

- Savoury and sweet spreads (such as sardine or chocolate)

- Prepared dips (such as cheese and chive or tikka)

- Slimmers' drinks and meal replacements.

Ingredients in food to watch out for

Here is a list of common food ingredients which could have come from a genetically modified crop. These ingredients are used widely in many of the processed foods we eat. Some of them, such as lecithin derived from soya, are used in as much as 60 per cent of all processed food products.

Obviously these ingredients could come from either a conventional crop or a genetically modified crop. But how can you tell which is which?

Labels are very little help. (For a more detailed explanation as to why this should be, read Part 2, 'Why you can't rely on labels'.) The net result is that only a few of the ingredients listed below would have to be labelled if they came from a genetically modified crop.

In the list that follows:

- Those ingredients that should be labelled by law are identified with an asterisk *****

- Those ingredients that may carry a voluntary label are identified with a letter 'v' in brackets **(v)**

- Those ingredients that do not need to be labelled have no symbol.

It is also important to appreciate that even asterisked ingredients do not need to be labelled if they are only present in insignificant quantities. For example, soya flour would have to be labelled as a general rule, but not if it was used only in very small amounts, as a 'flour improver' in bread, for example.

So when you see any of the ingredients below listed on a processed food, don't give them the benefit of the doubt. It is clear that there is a large supply of genetically modified soya, and to a lesser extent maize, available to food manufacturers. Some 30 per cent of the 1998 US soya harvest was genetically modified (a percentage that is predicted to rise in future years) and this has been deliberately mixed up with conventionally produced soya to make it difficult to trace.

This unsatisfactory situation means that

concerned consumers have no option but to operate a 'guilty until proven innocent policy' towards these ingredients when they shop. So avoid foods that contain these ingredients unless they are made by a company or brand with a clear-cut 'anti' genetically modified food stance. You can use the section 'Where the brands stand on GM food' to identify these brands.

AMERICAN TOMATO PASTE (V)

This is made from tomatoes with an antibiotic resistance gene grown in the US that have been genetically modified to make them slow-rotting. It is found in tubes and tins and in pizzas and Italian foods manufactured in the US.

CHEESE (V)

Most vegetarian, and some non-vegetarian, cheese, is curdled using chymosin – a genetically modified alternative to animal rennet. Only the Co-op voluntarily labels vegetarian cheese made with chymosin as 'genetically modified'.

SOYA BEANS, SOYA PIECES, SOYA SPROUTS *

Soya beans have been genetically modified to make them resistant to a herbicide. They can turn up in soya-based meals such as veggie burgers or veggie sausages.

SOYA FLOUR *
This turns up in nearly all typical British 'wrapped and sliced' loaves as well as in other bakery goods such as rolls, pikelets, scones, muffins and pizza bases. It is often used to make savoury extruded packet snacks for children and all kinds of biscuits, for example, caramel wafers.

SOYA PROTEIN AND SOYA PROTEIN ISOLATE *
Turns up in ready-mixed soya meals and other processed vegetarian foods such as veggie sausages and bean burgers, Pot Noodles and curries aimed at the convenience market, pies and pasties, infant cereals, frozen or chilled burgers and kievs, pâtés, meat and vegetarian spreads and savoury snacks.

TEXTURED VEGETABLE PROTEIN (TVP) *
Used as a substitute for meat in vegetarian mince and meat-mimicking processed vegetarian meals.

SOY SAUCE (SHOYU)
Made from fermented soy beans, this sauce is found throughout the oriental food repertoire in everything from Chinese and Thai-style ready-meals, through to larder standbys such as black bean and teriyaki sauce.

TOFU (BEANCURD)*
Made from soy beans, this is used in processed vegetarian foods and vegetarian dishes in oriental restaurants.

SOYA MILK *
Made from soy beans.

LECITHIN E322
This derivative of soya is one of the most common additives in food, where it is widely used as an emulsifier. It is extensively used in thousands of processed foods, including bread and bakery products, chocolate, margarine, cheese spread, mayonnaise, powdered milk and baby milk, milk drinks such as hot chocolate, slimmers' drinks, UHT and reduced-calorie cream, cheese spreads, fresh pasta, flans, mousses, cream desserts and ice-cream.

SOYA OIL
Used extensively in blended vegetable cooking oil, margarine, mayonnaise, salad dressings, sandwich spreads, ice-creams and frozen desserts, cheese replacements and cheese spreads, pizzas, tinned fish and granola-type breakfast cereals. It is often used as a lubricant to stop food sticking together in products such as ready-meal noodles. Dried fruits such as raisins are often oiled to prevent them from clumping together.

VEGETABLE COOKING OIL
Could contain soya oil (see above), or corn oil (see below).

MAIZE *
Some types of maize used for processing have been genetically modified to make them resistant to insects or herbicides. Some of these also contain an antibiotic-resistance gene. This maize is found in the form of tortilla chips and other corn snacks, Mexican-style taco shells, popcorn, and maize meal used for American Deep South dishes such as cornbread. It is thought that only a very small amount is currently grown in Europe, though this may increase. Most genetically modified maize is

being imported from the US. As yet, no 'sweet-corn' strains have been genetically modified, which means that, for the time being, fresh corn on the cob and processed corn such as niblets are not affected by genetic modification.

CORN OIL
Refined from maize, this can be found as a straight corn cooking oil, but can also be included in vegetable cooking oil blends, mayonnaise and salad dressings or used for any fried product from crisps through to 'crispy crumb' and 'battered' foods.

CORN SYRUP
This is refined from maize. It is sold on its own as a baking ingredient to be used as an alternative to golden or maple syrup. Used as a sweetener in confectionery (especially imports from the US), ice-cream and most soft, sweetened drinks.

DEXTROSE, GLUCOSE, MALTOSE, FRUCTOSE, SUCROSE (SYRUPS AND SOLIDS)
These sugars can all be processed from corn syrup. Extensively used in all kinds of sweet products, fruit and soft drinks such as colas.

MALTODEXTRIN

A low-cost, industrial carbohydrate filler which is derived from maize. This turns up in the most artificial processed foods such as gravy mixes and flavoured crisps. Also widely used in cooked processed meats such as sliced ham and chicken, and in dry baby foods.

XANTHAN GUM (E415)

Derived from corn sugar, this thickener is used in foods such as ice-cream, salad dressings and confectionery.

CORNFLOUR (CORNSTARCH)

This starch is refined from maize and is a ubiquitous ingredient in the British kitchen, where it is extensively used as a thickener. It is widely used by food manufacturers too, in products such as tinned baby food, fruit pie fillings, fruit drinks, cake mixes, fat-reduced products such as yogurt and crème fraîche, savoury sauce and sweet mousse mixes, oriental-style sauces (hoisin, oyster, yellow bean).

MODIFIED STARCH

This starch is usually refined from maize. It is used as an industrial thickener in processed foods such as wet baby food, 'thick'-type yogurts and low-fat 'lite' foods, sweet and savoury packet sauce mixes and cook-in and stir-fry type sauces.

HYDROLYSED VEGETABLE PROTEIN (HVP) OR HYDROLYSED SOYA PROTEIN

Amino acids often derived from soya which act as a flavour enhancer and give an almost 'meaty' taste. Used commonly in flavoured crisps and savoury extruded packet snacks, stock cubes and bouillon powder, savoury drinks and brine-injected meat such as cooked ham and chicken.

VEGETABLE FAT OR MARGARINE (HYDROGENATED AND UNHYDROGENATED)

May be manufactured from soy or corn oils. A ubiquitous ingredient in bread and bakery goods, cakes, biscuits and confectionery.

YEAST

Used in baking and brewing, both types of yeast can now be produced using genetic-engineering techniques. However, UK bakers and brewers say their industries do not use them. For more information, see the section 'Hidden genetic modification processes and the foods and drinks to which they are applied'.

ASPARTAME
This artificial sweetener can be made using a GM process. The company that makes aspartame for the UK market says it does not use this process. However, aspartame in products coming from the US could be made in this way.

FLAVOURINGS
Artificial flavourings can be produced using genetic-modification processes.

MILK PRODUCTS
A significant proportion of US milk is produced from cows injected with the GM growth hormone rBST. (For more information see the section 'Hidden genetic modification processes and the foods and drinks to which they are applied'.) Although this hormone is not approved for use in the EU, there is no ban on milk or milk products from the US that may have been produced with the aid of rBST. This means that the milk or milk products in any US food, for example confectionery or cake mixes, could have come from rBST-injected cows.

rBST milk could also find its way into products made in the EU. Although the EU has a milk surplus, and the liquid milk we drink is all produced locally, US milk products – such as skimmed milk powder, milk fat, whey powder, milk protein and lactose – can be sold in bulk to European food manufacturers.

Genetically modified foods in the pipeline

Many people find it hard to understand how, in practice, genetic modification affects the food we eat. This is mainly because the two key genetically modified crops we hear about at the moment are soya and maize. Since these are bulk commodity crops, most of us are not clear as to how they are used. We do not go out shopping and come back with a bag of soya flour or a sack of maize. Nor do we routinely scrutinise labels for obscure ingredients like soya protein isolate or modified starch.

In the next couple of years, however, our understanding looks set to sharpen as more genetically modified crops turn up in a whole, unprocessed form on our shelves. At present, only three GM crops – soya, maize and tomatoes – have been approved in the UK for consumption by humans. However there are many more waiting in the wings, either approved for growing (in field trials), for marketing, for seed production, or to be used as animal feed.

Literally hundreds of genes are being inserted into plants in field trials. In the US, field trials of fifty-six different plant species that have been genetically manipulated are complete. There have been 450 trials of thirty-two different genetic traits inserted into potatoes alone over an eight-year period. There are many more GM foods still at the experimental stage in laboratories throughout the world. The powerful transnational companies that have developed them are keen to see them on our shelves, so they can maximise their profits. They are knocking on the door of regulatory bodies, both in Europe and the UK, to get their products on to the market. So unless there is widespread consumer resistance to the first wave of GM foods, these pipeline experiments are likely to turn up in the fullness of time as the new genetically modified foods sitting on our shelves.

Here is a list of the genetically modified crops that are currently nearing commercialisation and that have already cleared many regulatory hurdles around the world:

Cherry tomatoes
Cotton (for oil)
Maize
Oil seed rape (for oil)
Papaya
Potatoes
Radicchio (red chicory salad leaf)
Squash
Sugar beet
Whole tomatoes

Hidden genetic modification processes and the foods and drinks to which they are applied

Many foods can be manufactured and processed using genetically modified products such as food additives, enzymes, hormones and flavourings. Some are genetically modified copies of a naturally occurring product such as riboflavin (vitamin B2), others are new products derived from genetically modified micro-organisms.

Because these products are classed as 'processing aids', they do not have to be listed on the label. The official rationale for this exemption is that because these products are only used to aid production, and are not present in the food we eventually eat, there is no need to worry. But this is no reassurance whatsoever. Even the most minute genetic tinkering in food processing could have devastating knock-on consequences, either for the environment, or for human health. Many people want to avoid any food or drink that has used genetic modification methods at any stage in its production or processing.

Unfortunately, it is impossible to know to what extent such products are used. Although they are licensed across a broad range of processed foods – everything from bread through fish and meat products to egg – no labelling is required and production methods are protected as commercial secrets.

Here's a taste of the hidden genetically modified products currently at the disposal of food and drink producers and manufacturers and some examples of the foods to which they may be applied.

BAKER'S YEAST
Since 1990 it has been legal to use genetically modified yeast. The yeast has been altered to speed up the production of enzymes responsible for dough fermentation. Genetically altered yeast may now be used in any food made using yeast. British bakers insist that it is not in commercial use but there are conflicting accounts from chefs who have had problems sourcing yeast with a genetic-modification-free guarantee.

BREWER'S YEAST
Since 1994, brewers have been able to use a genetically modified yeast – amylolytic yeast –

in the production of beer. It has had an enzyme added that makes it produce more alcohol. Any beer on the market could have been produced from this type of yeast. Like bakers, British brewers say that this yeast is only being used for 'developmental' purposes. But there are reports of imported beers being made using GM yeast.

Yeast extract is made from spent brewer's yeast. As well as being a popular spread, it is widely used in food processing as a salty flavouring, often turning up in products such as wet and dry baby food, crisps and savoury snacks, vegetarian products and sauces and pastes for cooking such as Thai curry paste.

RECOMBINANT BOVINE SOMATOTROPIN (rBST)

A genetically modified copy of a natural hormone in cows, it is injected into cows to make them produce more milk. This product is the subject of a moratorium in Europe which runs out in the millennium. Whether this European moratorium is extended or not, milk from cows treated with rBST has always been imported into the UK from the US.

So any US product which uses milk (ice-cream, cheese, frozen yogurt, confectionery, dried milk in sauce and cake mixes) could have come from rBST-injected cows.

TEST KIT FOR DETECTION OF ANTIBIOTIC RESIDUES

The streptococcus thermophilus micro-organism has been genetically modified in a test kit for the detection of antibiotic residues in the dairy industry.

RIBOFLAVIN (VITAMIN B2)

This vitamin can be produced synthetically using genetically modified *Bacillus subtilis*. It has been genetically altered to increase the bacteria production of riboflavin and an antibiotic (ampicillin) resistance marker has also been introduced.

Synthetic riboflavin is used to fortify or enhance the nutritional profile of many processed foods such as baby foods, breakfast cereals, fruit drinks and vitamin-enriched milk. It is also widely used in vitamin supplements.

CHYMOSIN

A GM substitute for animal rennet, it is used to curdle milk for hard cheese. Most vegetarian cheese and also much conventional cheese is made using this product.

FLAVOURINGS

Synthetic flavourings can be manufactured using genetic modification processes.

ALPHA AMYLASE
An enzyme which breaks down starch, thus producing more sugars for the starch to work on. It is used in the production of cereals and starch, soft and cola-type drinks, beer and wine.

HEMICELLULASE
Used by the baking industry to improve the strength of gluten in bread flour. Could be used in the production of any product made from bread flour.

LIPASE AND TRIACLYGLYCEROL
A genetically modified enzyme used to break down fats. Could be used in the manufacture of margarine, chocolate and any bakery item which contains fat.

OTHER GENETICALLY MODIFIED ENZYMES USED IN PROCESSED FOODS
Alpha-acetolate decarboxylase (beverages); catalase (milk and eggs); cyclodextrin-glucosyl transferase (cereals and starch); glucose iso-merase (cereals and starch); glucose oxidase (egg, beverages, bakery goods, salads); malto-genic amylase (starch and cereals, bakery products, beverages); pullulanase (starch); xylanase (bakery products).

Where the supermarkets stand on GM food

Until quite recently, UK supermarket chains were happy to go along tacitly, and in some cases, explicitly, with the biotech industry's push to get GM foods on our plates. When they first put GM tomato purée on their shelves, both Safeway and Sainsbury's made a great brouhaha about labelling it. But in common with other large food retailers, they otherwise appeared content to follow the feeble regulations which meant that most of the GM foods they stocked would not, in fact, be labelled. It was assumed that the UK public would swallow GM foods compliantly.

Iceland was the first chain to break ranks by declaring its own-brand products GM-free. And as public opinion further crystallised against GM food, the other large food retailers proceeded to flail around in various degrees of confusion, both concerning their general policy towards genetic modification and their labelling intentions.

Our supermarkets have now got the message that GM foods are a commercial disaster. They have all become more circumspect about nailing their colours to the GM mast because of the strength of consumer opposition. Most are saying that they are trying to minimise their use of GM ingredients to keep their customers happy and using this as a justification for deviating from their earlier conviction about the 'potential benefits' of GM food.

It is obvious that supermarket policy on GM food is still fluid and being made on the hoof. By choosing to support the chains with more robust anti-GM policies, consumers can push the waverers to abandon any lingering commitment to GM food.

Below, you will find an analysis of where the supermarkets and other food retailers stand on GM food. This is based on statements supplied by them and other public information about their intentions. The supermarkets are ranked* on a sliding scale from best (most negative about GM food) to worst (most in favour of . GM food).

* This ranking is liable to change as supermarket policy is in flux.

Best to worst on GM food

ICELAND

In February 1998, this frozen-food retailer announced that from 1 May that year, none of its own-label produce would contain any GM ingredients. What's more, Iceland uses the term 'ingredient' in an all-embracing way to cover derivatives of GM crops, not just ingredients that would need to be labelled by law.

This was a brave move for a chain that traditionally services a price-sensitive clientele buying a preponderance of processed food where the use of ingredients derived from GM crops is ubiquitous. Iceland offers refreshing clarity on the GM issue, saying 'the introduction of GM ingredients is probably the most significant and potentially dangerous development in the food industry this century'. The chain's chief executive is a passionate and committed opponent of GM foods.

Verdict: Unequivocal and principled in its opposition to genetic modification, Iceland did consumers a service by showing that it was possible to eliminate GM ingredients in own-label products by sourcing 'identity-preserved' non-GM supplies.

MARKS & SPENCER

Not so long ago, M&S stated categorically that GM food was simply not an issue for its customers. It promptly got a shock when those same customers told it otherwise. Almost overnight, M&S moved from its initial pro-GM food position. Now it has undertaken to remove all GM ingredients and their derivatives from its food by the end of June 1999. Since M&S food halls are 100 per cent own-brand, this will leave St Michael in the enviable position of being the only retailer that can say with confidence that it is a GM-free zone. 'We have to put our customers first and we made this decision as a direct result of listening carefully to their views.'

Verdict: Once full of the joys of GM, M&S's about-turn shows just how influential consumers can be when they flex their muscles.

ASDA

This chain took steps early on to remove GM material from its own-brand products, replacing them with ingredients from certified 'non-GM' sources, or reformulating the products. It says that by the end of summer 1999 'it is likely' that none of its products will contain ingredients from GM sources. At the same time Asda asserts that, following 'rigorous testing' before being introduced, the GM soya and maize protein in its products is 'safe to eat' – thus trying to have it both ways. It also takes up a position on the environmental front by saying it believes that it was unacceptable that US growers 'failed to segregate genetically modified soya at harvest from conventionally produced supplies'.

Verdict: Asda has gained a public profile as an anti-GM company and has clearly taken the view that by coming out strongly against GM products it will gain, not lose, customer loyalty.

SAINSBURY'S
This chain took a bit of a pounding because of its family connections with the biotech industry. The chain's own David Sainsbury – also the Government's science minister – is on record as being pro-GM. In the past, Sainsbury's supermarket chain has pioneered GM foods such as tomato paste and waxed lyrical about the potential benefits of genetic modification.

Now Sainsbury's has set up an international consortium of food retailers and industry members whose job is to establish validated sources of GM-free ingredients and their derivatives in order to 'give UK shoppers what they want'. In the meantime, Sainsbury's is on record as having a 'commitment to eliminate GM from its own brand products . . . these will be discontinued if a GM-free alternative cannot be found'.

Verdict: A jaw-dropping policy rethink from this chain. It shows once more how consumers can call the shots if they are vocal enough.

SUPERQUINN

This Irish chain has decided to remove GM ingredients from its own-brand foods. It is part of the international consortium of super-markets committed to establishing validated sources of 'identity-preserved' GM-free ingredients and their derivatives. 'We do not see it as a food safety issue, but as a customer issue. Our customers don't want GM food.'

Verdict: The leading Irish supermarket group has responded to the intense opposition to GM food and crops in Ireland in its usual dynamic fashion.

WAITROSE

The south-east England chain is in the enviable position of being able to say that it has proactively removed soya from its products or replaced GM soya with soya from 'non-GM' crops. The result is that no Waitrose products contain GM 'ingredients', as defined by law. It does, however, still stock foods with derivatives of GM crops such as soya oil and lecithin and intends to label these in time. It reports that it is now 'making good progress in identifying the sources of soya and maize from "traditional" crops'.

Philosophically, Waitrose appears to be in favour of genetic modification, saying in its customer leaflet that this technology could improve crop yields, produce new varieties with nutrition benefits and reduce the use of chemicals. Waitrose notes consumer-safety concerns about GM foods but takes no view on them.

Verdict: Another upmarket chain distancing itself from GM foods as fast as it can.

CO-OP (CWS)
In its literature for customers, the Co-op used to brim over with enthusiasm for genetic modification of food. Now it says, 'Our aim is to eliminate from our products, ingredients and additives of GM origin. However, in excep-

tional circumstances, and by agreement on a case-by-case basis, we will accept GM-derived ingredients in Co-op brands. The supplier must convince us that neither reformulation nor segregated (GM-free) sources are commercially viable. Our policy is then to label each and every ingredient and additive.' This undertaking is consistent with its long-standing 'Right To Know' labelling policy: it is the only chain to label cheese made with chymosin as GM.

Of late, the Co-op has been lobbying government for a precautionary approach and for the traceability of raw materials (such as soya beans) and processed products. The Co-op notes some environmental reasons why consumers might want to avoid GM foods, citing the possible transfer of a modified genetic trait to wild species and weeds and the use of antibiotic-resistant marker genes in GM food.

Verdict: The Co-op has reacted to consumer opposition by actively lobbying government and business for a precautionary approach. It has maintained its straightforward and open approach to labelling too.

SOMERFIELD / KWIKSAVE/ GATEWAY

This group likes to make matters clear. 'We have looked at all the products in our own-label range containing soya to see if alternative ingredients can be used. Where this is not possible, we have asked suppliers to source "identity-preserved" soya that is free from genetic modification. Where that is not possible, we will always label that product.'

The group publicly expresses frustration at the US Government's refusal to enforce the segregation of GM soya and seems to feel that UK food manufacturers are being dictated to by US growers of GM crops.

Verdict: This group does not appear to see any benefits in GM food and is actively trying to minimise its involvement with GM ingredients.

WM MORRISON

This north of England chain shows a certain northern canniness towards genetic modification. It points out this technology is 'still in the early stages of development' and says it will 'monitor the latest scientific research'. Morrison's is currently looking into the feasibility of reformulating products to avoid GM ingredients and of sourcing GM-free foods in future.

Verdict: A chain refreshingly free from gung-ho pro-GM reassurance, Wm Morrison reflects its consumers' concerns. This chain is positioning itself at arm's length from GM food.

BOOTHS

This north-west of England chain says that its own-label food is GM-free 'as far as we are able to ascertain'. 'Due to the lack of a cohesive national/EU policy for the food industry, it is difficult for our company to draw conclusions as to whether or not the use of gene technology in food production is likely to have an adverse effect on the environment and the health and well-being of our customers.'

Verdict: More reticence from the north-west. Booths sounds distinctly underwhelmed by genetic modification but isn't going to get militant about it.

TESCO

Tesco has never actively championed GM food and has recently toned down its muted support for biotechnology. Last year it was 'cautiously welcoming the advantages offered by genetic modification' and appearing confident that its customers would trust both the judgement of Tesco and the safety regulators to protect them from harm. Of late this optimism has given way to brief statements about extending its voluntary labelling of ingredients derived from GM crops in tandem with assurances that 'product safety is our prime concern'.

Verdict: Tesco is sitting on the fence and keeping its head well down. It is staying clear of the public debate, but as the UK's largest retailer, it could be pushed into firming up its position to take more account of consumer opposition to GM food.

SAFEWAY

In its customer leaflet, Safeway sets out to seduce its customers into believing that GM crops are a 'good thing' by defining them as crops which have 'improved characteristics'. It then goes on to assure us that the only GM products it sells are those which offer 'tangible benefits' – to whom, it does not say – and that in its own-brand products it will 'minimise' the use of any products which do not have demonstrable 'advantages'. It also assures customers that there is no reason for them to avoid foods containing GM ingredients since they have been passed as safe to eat by 'the appropriate UK and international regulatory authorities'.

Verdict: Actively defends GM foods and puts trust in declarations of 'safety' by regulatory authorities. Thus, well out of step with increasing consumer concern.

Best to worst on organic alternatives

The single simplest way to avoid GM food is to buy organic food: organic food rules outlaw genetic modification of any kind. So, in an ideal world, what most anti-GM food shoppers would like is to be able to shop in a supermarket with no GM food and lots of organic food.

It is therefore both irritating and ironic that the chains currently on record as being most opposed to or wary about GM food are generally rather poor performers when it comes to stocking organic lines. There is an explanation for this: the most anti-GM food chains traditionally cater for a cost-conscious market which relies on cheaper, processed food. Within the processed food category, there is simply less organic food around and organic prices are generally higher, so it is harder for price-driven chains to develop an organic range.

At present, three chains are slugging it out to have the biggest portfolio of organic foods. These are:

- Sainsbury's (over 400 organic lines)

- Waitrose (over 300 organic lines)

- Tesco (over 200 organic lines).

All other chains are well behind these three but are making efforts to make up some of the ground they have lost and significantly extend their range. Marks & Spencer, for example, once extremely sceptical about the future for organic food, has recently introduced a quite impressive organic food chill counter in its larger stores.

Even if you do have a supermarket in your area which does have a reasonable supply of organic food, it is worth bearing in mind that nowadays there are other more direct and convenient ways to buy organic food. Obviously you can get it from an organic food or farm shop, but there are now quite a few home-delivery and 'box' schemes operated by either growers or intermediate distributors.

The best way to tap into organic supplies in your area is to get a copy of the Soil Association's 'Where to Buy Organic Food' book. See the listing for this organisation in the section 'Where to find out more about genetically modified food'.

Where the brands stand on GM food

You can use this section to get more information about 'branded' foods. 'Branded' means that they are not 'own label'. 'Own label' means that they are specific to a certain supermarket or food chain. (For information about own-brands see 'Where the supermarkets stand on GM food' and the 'Directory'.)

This section looks at familiar branded foods you buy that could be genetically modified or become so in the near future. It gives each brand a red/ amber/ green rating*.

Green The company never knowingly sources genetically modified ingredients or derivatives. Its foods are highly unlikely to contain GM

* This rating is based on policy and statements of intent supplied by the company or its parent company. It is not possible to verify these claims independently and therefore they should not be interpreted as being certified by this guide.

ingredients or derivatives and would only do so through unintentional contamination.

Amber The company's foods could be genetically modified. Companies in this category have no clear stance for or against genetic modification. They either cannot guarantee all their products or can only give a qualified GM-free guarantee 'for the time being'.

Red The company sees some potential benefits in GM food and is prepared to use GM ingredients and derivatives. Its foods are more likely to contain GM ingredients and derivatives.

Brands are listed alphabetically. Where the brand is less well-known, examples of some, but not all, of its products are given to help recognition.

The green brands
(A mixture of wholefood brands and better-known household name brands)

Advantage breakfast cereal
Allos (breakfast cereals, pastas, spreads)
Amaizin tortilla chips
Ambrosia
Aspall apple juice

Baby Organix baby food
Bahlsen biscuits
Barbagallo pasta
Barley Cup
Ben & Jerry's ice-cream
Bensons crisps (salted, unflavoured only)
Billington's sugar
Bio Aras (olive oil, olives and spreads)
Biokorn biscuits
Biona (grains, cereals, pizza, mayonnaise)
Bionova (jams, purées, bottled vegetables)
Biotta juices
Bio Verde pasta
Blue Dragon (oriental foods)
Bonsoy soya milk
Bonvita (rice cakes, confectionery)
Bounty bars and ice-cream
Bovril
Broadlands vegetable suet
Brown & Polson
Burger Knacke crispbreads
Campo (pasta sauces, tinned tomatoes)
Carriba snack bars
Carr's biscuits
Caterplan
Cawston Vale fruit juice
Celebrations chocolates
Cereal Terra (Italian condiments)

Chalice (olive pâtés, salad dressing)
Charbonnel & Walker chocolate
Cheeselets
Chocolate Ready breakfast cereal
Chocoreale confectionery
Clearspring (Japanese foods)
Coles Traditional Christmas Pudding
Community Foods (grains, pulses, dried fruit, nuts)
Cornflower (butter, cheese)
Cow & Gate milks and foods
Crazy Jack (grains, pulses, dried fruit, nuts)
Crawford's biscuits
Crunchy Bran breakfast cereal
Cypressa (olives, tahini)
Daddies sauce
DCL active dried yeast
De Rit (biscuits, sauces, spreads)
Direct Foods (soya products)
Divine chocolate
Doves Farm (flour, biscuits, cereals)
Dragonfly (tofu, tofu burgers)
Duchesse spreads
Emile Noel oils
Essential Trading (grains, pulses, dried fruit, nuts)
Evernat (biscuits, pasta)
Familia

Family Circle biscuits
Flyte wafers and ice-cream
From Soya
Galaxy chocolate
Galloway cheese
Galbani (Italian products)
Go Organic (soups, sauces)
Granose (margarine and spreads)
Granovita
Green and Black's (chocolate, ice-cream)
Green City Wholefoods (grains, pulses, dried
    fruit, nuts)
Grizzly confectionery
Gusto soft drink
Haldane (soya and vegetarian products)
Hellenic
Hellman's
Hipp baby food
Holland and Barrett (foods only, not
    supplements)
HP
Huileries de Berry oils
I Hate Marmite
Infinity Foods
Johannusmolen (savoury and soup mixes)
Hovis cracker
Jacob's biscuits (sweet and savoury), crackers
    and toasts

Joosters sweets
Jordans
Kallo stocks
Karyatis (olives, oils)
Kellogg's cereals (all types)
Kettle Foods (chips, poppins, tortilla chips)
Kitchen Garden (TVP, savoury pastes)
Knorr
KP snacks
KTC edibles (fats, oils, drinks, sauces, spreads)
La Bio-Idea (Italian products)
La Terra e il Cielo (Italian products)
Langdales essences
Lesieur
Lima cereals
Linda McCartney
Lindt chocolate
Lockets sweets
London Herb & Spice Co
Lye Cross cheese
Maltesers
M&M's
Marmite
Marriage's flour
Marigold stocks
Mars bars, drinks and ice-cream
Marshalls (all breakfast cereals except
    Marshalls Fruit)

Martlet (jams, chutneys, syrups)
Mazola
McCain (except Humdingers range)
MacSween haggis
McVitie's biscuits
Mennucci (Italian products)
Meridian Foods (oils, spreads, jams)
Micro Rice
Milky Way
Milupa milks and foods
Minstrels
Molenaartje biscuits
Mornflake breakfast cereals
Mr Brain's
My Mate Marmite
Napolina
Ocean Spray (cranberry products)
Paterson's biscuits
Plamil (chocolate, soya drinks)
Peak Frean biscuits
Phileas Fogg
Pot Mash
Prewetts (biscuits, cakes)
Pringles
Prosoya/So Nice
Provamel (soya milk, desserts)
Quorn pieces
Rachel's Dairy yogurt

Rajah
Rapunzel (biscuits, confectionery)
Readybrek
Realeat (vegetarian products)
Revels
Ripple
Ritz biscuits
Rocombe Farm ice-cream
Ross (burgers, sausages, processed foods)
R&R Tofu
Rowse (spreads, sauces, syrups)
Sanchi (oriental foods)
San Marco pizza
Savex
Sesame Snaps
Shepherdboy confectionery
Shipton Mills flour
Singletons Dairy cheese
Silver Spoon sugar
Skittles sweets and fruit ice
Snickers bars and ice-cream
Sojasun
Soya Health Foods Ltd
Soya Kass
Spangles lolly
Spread the Word
Stamp Collection (savoury snacks, confectionery, flour)

Starburst sweets and ice-cream
Stute jams
Suma Foods (cereals, pulses, dried fruit, nuts)
Sunny Delight
Sunita (halva, peanut butter, tahini)
Swedish Glace ice desserts
Taifun (tofu products)
Tastebreaks
Terresana (beans, corn chips)
Thorntons chocolates
Tofutti (dairy substitutes)
Tomatina
Topic bars and ice-cream
Tracker bars
Trio biscuits
Twiglets
Tunes
Twix bars and ice-cream
Unisoy
Valfrutta (Italian products)
Vegimince
Village Bakery
Vitalinea bars
Viver (pasta sauce)
Warburtons
Weetabix (all types, except Weetabix Fruit)
Whole Earth Foods (breakfast cereals, spreads,
    tinned food)

Yeatex
Yeo Valley yogurt
Yesta
Yum Tums cakes and biscuits
Zest Foods (sauces, salad dressings)

The amber brands
All Gold confectionery
Allinson bread
Amoy
Angel Delight
Atora
Bagel Bites
Barker & Dobson sweets
Barratt's sweets
Baxters soup
Birds Custard
Bisto
Boboli (pizza, flat breads)
Brannigans crisps
Buitoni
Butterkist
Cadbury's Cakes
Callard & Bowser
Cauldron (tofu, tofu burgers, vegetarian pâtés)
Cheddarie
Choc Dips
Clarnico sweets

Côte d'Or confectionery
Cracker Barrel cheese
Dairylea spread
Doritos
Dunkers
First Choice bread mixes
Granary
Hales (cakes)
Heinz
Highbran bread
Hovis
Jameson's sweets
Keiller sweets
Kingsmill
Kraft (cheese, dressings)
Lanes (Vecon)
Lyons Cakes
Maynard's sweets
McCain Humdingers range
McDougall's
Mellow Birds
Mighty White bread
Monster Munch
Mother's Pride
Mr Kipling cakes
Nimble
Nuttalls
Pataks

Paxo
Penguin biscuits
Philadelphia cheese
Princes
Quavers
Rank Hovis Granary
Rose's Lime
Salt 'n' Shake
Savoury Moments
Schweppes soft drinks
Sharps sweets
Smith's crisps
Square crisps
Sunblest
Sunkist
Tate & Lyle
Terry's confectionery
Toblerone
Traidcraft (chocolate, jams, nuts)
Trex
Tudor crisps
Walkers crisps
Whitworths
Wilkinson sweets

The red brands

Aero
After Eight

Allora
Alpen (all types)
Astros
Batchelors
Bird's Eye Walls
Black Magic
Blue Band
Boost
Bowyers sausages
Branston pickle
Cadbury's chocolate
Caramel and Caramello
Chicken Tonight
Chomp
Coffee-Mate and Tea-Mate
Colman's
Cookeen
Contrast
Crisp 'n' Dry
Crosse & Blackwell
Crunchy
Curly Wurly
Dalepak
Darkness
Delight
Double Decker
Echo
Elmlea

Fab lollipops
Flake
Flora
Fox's biscuits
Fox's glacier mints
Freddo
Fry
Fry's confectionery
Fruitibix
Fuse
Gale's
Golden Crisp
Golden Wonder crisps
I Can't Believe It's Not Butter
Inspirations
Kit-Kat
Krona
Marble
Marshalls fruit cereal
Matchmakers
Maverick
Milk Tray
Milkybar
Mint Leaves
Mr Men ices
Mirage ices
Mivvis
Nescafé cappuccino

Nesquick
OK sauces
Old Jamaica
Olivio
Outline
Oxo
Paynes confectionery
Peperami
Picnic
Polo
Pork Farms
Pot Noodle
Pretzel Flips
Pura oils, margarines and spreads
Quality Street
Ragu
Rolo
Roses chocolates
Ross
Rowntree's jelly
Rowntree's fruit pastilles
Ruffle
Sarson's pickles and relishes
Sharwoods
Spry Crisp 'n' Dry
Stork
Summer County
Swiss Chalet confectionery

Toffee Crisp
Smarties
Spar
Spira
Star Bar
St Ivel
Taz
Tiffin
Time Out
Twirl
Velvet Mint
Vesta
Waistline (Nestlé)
Walnut Whip
Weetabix fruit cereal
Weetos
White Cap
White Flora
Wispa
Yorkie
Zoom ices

Your shopping basket profile and the GM risk

Have you ever stood in a supermarket queue and analysed the contents of the baskets and trolleys around you? In this section, you'll find profiles of certain common types of shopping-basket contents and an analysis of how likely each one is to contain genetically modified ingredients.

The unprocessed/healthy/organic basket

Organic beef

Milk

A mixture of conventional and organic fruit and vegetables

Free-range chicken (whole) and eggs

Fresh fish

Cheddar cheese

Low-fat fruit yogurt

Muesli

Stoneground wholemeal bread

This basket avoids most GM foods. All the organic items are guaranteed to be free from genetic modification. The whole, unprocessed, free-range chicken, eggs and fish are not yet categories of food affected by genetic modification. However, other items are problematical.

British milk is safe from genetic modification until the millennium. But from 2001, it could come from cows injected with the GM growth hormone, rBST. There is a good chance that the cheese has been made with chymosin, the GM equivalent of traditional rennet. The fruit yogurt could have been flavoured with a GM flavouring, be thickened with corn starch or sweetened with sugars derived from GM corn.

The raisins in the muesli could have been coated with GM soya oil to stop them sticking together. The bread sounds wholesome, but if it is a typical British 'wrapped and sliced' loaf, the wheat may have been broken down using GM enzymes. The loaf is likely to contain vegetable fat which could come from GM soya or maize. It could also have been made using GM yeast. British bakers say they use only traditional yeast, but the law does allow them to use the GM kind.

The 'too busy working' basket

All-day-breakfast sandwich

Chargrilled chicken slices

Breaded red pepper strips

Authentic Chinese-style whole aromatic
crispy duck

French dressing

Bite-sized prepared appetisers

Cheese and chive dip

Tortilla chips

Spicy potato wedges

Every item in this basket is likely to contain a GM ingredient unless it comes from a brand which is organic or gives a 'No GM ingredients' guarantee on the label. The tortilla chips are likely to be made from GM maize and all the other items could contain soya in one form or another. GM maize could also crop up again as modified starch in the soup.

The 'can't cook won't cook' basket

Tinned chicken soup

Chinese sweet-and-sour pork ready meal

Lasagne ready meal

Hickory smoked pork ribs

Onion bhajis

Instant cheese sauce packet

Lattice pork pie

Triple decker pizza

Chicken quarter-pounders in bun

With its emphasis on quick convenience foods which are heavily processed, every item in this basket could contain GM soya in various forms. The pork, lasagne, bhajis and pizza are also likely to have oil or sugars from GM maize.

The children's basket

Thin and crispy cheese and tomato pizza

Chocolate spread

Tinned tomato soup

Fish bites

Sausage rolls

Crunchy crumb chicken dippers

Microwavable beefburgers

Cheesy potato nuggets

Chipolata sausages

As prime consumers of heavily processed junk food, children are in the front line for GM food. Eating a typical 'children's food' repertoire as above, they would be likely to swallow a cocktail of food ingredients from GM crops.

The vegetarian basket

Veggie burgers

Soya mince

Tofu

Margarine/spread

Vegetarian cheddar cheese

Peanut butter

Yeast extract

Spinach and ricotta cannelloni ready meal

Pasta and cheese salad snack bowl

Unless the veggie burgers, soya mince and tofu come from an organic or 'No GM ingredients' brand, these items are extremely likely to come from GM soya, especially if they are bought from a supermarket rather than a wholefood shop. The margarine/spread, the peanut butter, the cannelloni and salad bowl are likely to contain oils, thickeners and emulsifiers from GM soya or maize. The cheese is made with chymosin, the GM substitute for rennet. The yeast extract is derived from brewer's yeast, which can legally be made using a GM process.

The foodie basket

Polenta or cornbread maize flour

US 'premium' ice-cream

Tomato paste purée

High cocoa solids dark chocolate

Hoisin sauce

Fructose

Prepared sushi

Thai curry paste

Chilled fresh egg noodles

Unless it comes from an organic or 'No GM ingredients' brand, the maize flour could come from a GM crop. US milk is widely produced by injecting cows with the GM growth hormone, rBST. The tomato paste purée could be from GM tomatoes. The lecithin in the chocolate is very likely to come from GM soya. The sugars in the hoisin sauce and the fructose could both be derived from GM maize. The curry paste is likely to contain GM soya or corn oil in 'vegetable oil' and the noodles could be coated in it too. The soy sauce that comes with the sushi could be GM.

Baby food ingredients to look out for

Many parents are particularly anxious to avoid giving their babies foods that could contain ingredients or derivatives from a GM crop. This is not only because they do not want their children to be part of a genetic experiment, but also because there is concern that the use of GM soya could increase the incidence of allergy to soya amongst children.

Any of the following ingredients in baby food could have been derived from either GM soya or maize. None of them would have to be labelled by law. In addition, they are all indicators of baby food that has been overprocessed. None of these ingredients is necessary in a good-quality product relying on the best raw materials. They are used either as bulking agents, flavourings, emulsifiers or, in the case of vitamins, to give the product an aura of health. GM or not GM, your baby will be better off without them.

In infant formula milk
Soya lecithin
Vegetable oil
Vitamin B2

In 'wet' food in jars

Cornflour
Modified cornflour
HVP
Lecithin
Soya flour
Vitamin B2
Yeast products

In 'dry' baby foods in packets

HVP
Hydrogenated vegetable fat
Lecithin
Maltodextrin
Soya flour
Soya protein isolate
Vegetable fat
Vitamin B2
Yeast products

Where the baby food brands stand

Each baby food brand has been given an amber or green rating*.

Green The company never knowingly sources genetically modified ingredients or uses GM processing aids.

Amber The company's foods could contain genetically modified ingredients or their derivatives. Companies in this category cannot give a robust GM-free guarantee and have no clear stance for or against the use of GM ingredients in baby food.

* This rating is based on policy and statements of intent supplied by the company or its parent company. It is not possible to verify these claims independently and therefore they should not be interpreted as being certified by this guide.

Green baby food brands
Baby Organix
Cow & Gate
Hipp
Milupa
Olvarit

Amber baby food brands
Boots
Farley
SMA

Part 4

Directory of supermarket foods with GM labels

This directory lists supermarket own-brand products with ingredients that have been labelled* as genetically modified. It will alert you to the types of food most likely to contain GM ingredients and their derivatives.

Supermarkets are currently trying to minimise or, in some cases, eliminate GM ingredients from their own-brand range by reformulating or delisting products. It is therefore likely that the number of entries in this directory will shrink in future.

Prepared poultry-based products and meals

Tesco southern fried chicken nuggets (frozen)
Tesco crunchy crumb chicken (frozen)
Tesco oriental stir fry
Tesco hot and spicy chicken wings
Tesco chicken in red pepper sauce and
    vegetables
Tesco chicken spring rolls
Tesco sweet and sour chicken
Tesco chicken in black bean sauce
Tesco chicken chow mein
Tesco chicken satay
Tesco Peking duck rice bowl

*Products appearing on this list have been labelled as genetically modified in the two months preceding publication of this guide.

Tesco Chinese meal for 1/2
Tesco southern fried chicken portions
Tesco Louisiana stir fry
Tesco hot and spicy basted chicken breasts
Tesco Thai basted chicken breasts
Tesco barbecued chicken breasts
Tesco Mediterranean basted chicken breasts
Tesco plum and chilli glazed chicken breasts
Tesco breaded chicken steaks
Tesco lime and coriander chicken kievs
Tesco chicken tikka thigh bites
Tesco chicken rigate in creamy basil sauce
Tesco chicken and cashew nuts
Tesco Kung po chicken
Tesco Mexican chicken enchilada
Tesco roast chicken filled Yorkshire pudding
Tesco 95% fat-free Hunan chicken rice bowl
Texco 97% fat-free chicken in white wine
Tesco chicken in red wine
Tesco chicken jalfrezi
Tesco chicken balti
Tesco chicken korma
Tesco Indian meal for 2
Tesco butter chicken
Tesco chicken saag
Tesco chicken curry and rice
Tesco tikka chapati pack
Tesco chicken and cashew nuts

Tesco duck in pineapple and plum sauce

Tesco New Orleans chicken and prawn gumbo

Sainsbury's buffalo-style chicken wings

Sainsbury's chargrilled chicken fillets with olive oil, lemon grass and coconut

Sainsbury's fresh Gressingham duck 2 breast fillets with zesty orange sauce

Sainsbury's authentic Chinese-style 2 crispy duck legs (with pancakes and hoisin sauce)

Sainsbury's authentic Chinese-style whole aromatic crispy duck

Sainsbury's chicken fillets with lemon and pepper

Safeway chicken dippers (battered and breaded) (frozen)

Safeway breaded chicken nuggets (frozen)

Safeway breaded chicken nibbles (frozen)

Safeway breaded southern fried chicken nuggets (frozen)

Safeway sun, moon and stars breaded shapes

Safeway chicken cordon bleu kievs (frozen)

Safeway chicken kievs (frozen)

Safeway chicken kievs lemon and tarragon (frozen)

Safeway chicken kievs tikka masala (frozen)

Safeway chicken breast fillets in southern fried crunchy crumb coating (frozen)

Safeway chicken breast fillets in crispy batter
(frozen)
Safeway chicken burgers (frozen)
Safeway breaded chicken nibbles (frozen)
Safeway invitations chicken goujons
Safeway sweet-and-sour chicken with fried
egg
Safeway chicken and black bean sauce with
egg-fried rice
Safeway chicken and cashew nuts with egg-
fried rice
Safeway chicken and Chinese mushrooms with
egg-fried rice
Safeway spicy chicken wrap
Safeway chicken quarter-pounders with bun
Safeway lemon and pepper chicken drumsticks
and thighs
Safeway chicken fillets in creamy Dijon and
dill sauce
Safeway chicken kiev with cream cheese and
chives
Safeway chicken kiev with lemon and tarragon
Safeway chicken fillets in sun-dried tomato
sauce
Safeway chicken fillets in balti-style sauce
Safeway cooked chicken – mini chicken fillets
Safeway turkey breast escalopes – lemon and
pepper

Safeway sizzler chicken wings in Chinese-style marinade

Safeway sizzler turkey kebab southern-fried

Safeway sizzler turkey kebab hot and spicy

Safeway sizzler chicken drumsticks with sweet chilli and sesame seed seasoning

Safeway sizzler chicken wings – chilli and tomato

Asda chicken in black bean sauce

Asda chicken in black bean sauce with rice

Asda chicken and black bean

Asda Chinese meal for one (banquet for one)

Asda southern-fried chicken (frozen and not frozen)

Asda chicken animal shapes (frozen)

Asda battered chicken dippers (frozen)

M&S chargrilled breast of chicken slices

M&S flame-grilled spicy chicken fillets with rice

M&S cured breast of chicken slices

M&S crispy battered chicken

M&S crispy aromatic duck

M&S roast duck in plum sauce

M&S steamers chicken and Chinese vegetables

M&S steamers chicken and chilli

M&S Chinese-style chicken mini fillets

M&S chicken chow mein

M&S chicken and black bean with Chinese-style rice

M&S sweet-and-sour chicken with rice

M&S Chinese oriental vegetables with Chinese-style rice

M&S Cantonese chicken rice bowl

Co-op savoury rice – chicken flavour

Co-op chicken and mushroom slices

Co-op chicken in black bean sauce

Co-op roast chicken tikka nuggets

Co-op hot and spicy Mexican-style roast chicken drumsticks

Co-op rosemary and garlic turkey breast steaks

Co-op Mediterranean-style tomato and garlic turkey breast steaks

Co-op chicken drumsticks coated in a Chinese-style seasoning

Co-op chicken thighs coated in a Chinese-style seasoning

Co-op chicken drumsticks coated in a hickory smoke flavour seasoning

Co-op chicken thighs coated in a hickory smoke flavour seasoning

Co-op chicken nuggets breaded

Co-op chicken nuggets battered

Co-op chicken thighs coated in a Mexican-flavour seasoning

Co-op chicken drumsticks coated in a
  Mexican-flavour seasoning
Co-op chicken kievs cheese and ham
Somerfield homestyle roast chicken casserole
  and herb dumplings
Somerfield six turkey drumstick shapes
Somerfield breaded chicken burgers
Somerfield chargrilled chicken tikka
Somerfield chargrilled lemon chicken
Somerfield chargrilled chicken with
  mayonnaise, red pepper
Somerfield chicken with chestnut stuffing,
  mayonnaise etc.
Somerfield lattice slice, roast chicken and
  broccoli
Somerfield smoked turkey, sausage and
  cranberry sauce
Somerfield the deep south chicken wing
  selection
Somerfield barbeque chicken
Somerfield turkey and bacon loaf
Somerfield turkey and chicken sausages
Somerfield chicken curry
Waitrose chicken goujons
Waitrose chicken breast fillets
Waitrose chicken bites
Morrisons chicken burgers

Prepared meat-based products and meals

Tesco mushroom and bacon crunchies

Tesco cheese, leek and bacon crunchies

Tesco meat loaf

Tesco sweet and sour

Tesco battered sweet and sour pork

Tesco Chinese meal for 1/2

Tesco Cantonese pork rice bowl

Tesco Shanghai beef rice bowl

Tesco hamburger in a bun (frozen)

Tesco beefburgers with onion (frozen)

Tesco cannelloni (frozen)

Tesco lasagne (frozen)

Tesco sliced beef in gravy (frozen)

Tesco value sausages

Tesco value chipolata sausages

Tesco Butchers range pork and beef sausages

Tesco braised pork joint with apple and
cider gravy

Tesco 95% fat-free lasagne

Tesco 97% fat-free steak chasseur

Tesco pork stroganoff

Tesco vindaloo

Tesco lamb roghan josh and rice

Tesco korma and pilau rice

Tesco lamb methi

Tesco beef cannelloni

Tesco cannelloni
Tesco spaghetti amatriciana
Sainsbury's microwavable beef burgers
Sainsbury's microwavable quarter-pounders
Safeway sausages (frozen)
Safeway pork cocktail sausages (frozen)
Safeway sizzlers lamb shoulder chops with
  mint coating
Safeway easy roast pork joint with sunflower
  oil and herbs
Safeway easy roast pork joint with seasoned
  pork and mustard stuffing
Safeway easy roast pork joint with seasoned
  port and mushroom stuffing
Asda farm stores chilli con carne
Asda spaghetti bolognese
Asda chorizos
Asda Cumberland vegetable sausages
Asda meaty vegetable sausages
M&S Aberdeen Angus beef sausages
M&S crispy chilli beef
M&S Chinese take-away box
Co-op sausage casserole
Co-op ham, cheese and mushroom slice
Co-op beef curry with rice (frozen)
Co-op ground lamb grills
Co-op ground beef grills
Co-op ground pork grills

Co-op chargrilled beef burgers
Co-op chargrilled pork burgers
Co-op hot and spicy Mexican-flavour pork ribs
Co-op hickory smoke flavour pork ribs
Co-op hickory smoke flavour shoulder steaks
Co-op hickory smoke flavour pork shoulder
   steaks
Co-op pork ribs in a hickory-flavour coating
Co-op pork ribs in a Mexican-style coating
Co-op pork ribs in a Chinese-style coating
Co-op sausage, beans and mash
Co-op meat loaf
Co-op thick pork and beef sausages
Co-op spicy beef and pepperoni ravioli
Somerfield four beef olives
Somerfield butcher's choice Glamorgan
   sausages
Somerfield fried onion and cheese pork
   sausages
Somerfield pork and herb sausages
Somerfield celebrations cooked cocktail
   sausages
Somerfield cocktail sausage selection pack
Somerfield homestyle sausages in red wine
Somerfield lamb noisettes with black pudding
Somerfield Lincolnshire sausage meat
Somerfield liver sausage
Somerfield pork and leek sausage

Somerfield pork and tomato sausage
Somerfield premium variety cocktail sausages
Somerfield Yorkshire pudding, sausage and
   onion
Somerfield Lincolnshire sausages (frozen)
Somerfield basics economy burgers with onion
   (frozen)
Somerfield bacon streakies
Somerfield classic lasagne
Somerfield ham, mushroom tagliatelle

Pies, sausage rolls, pasties, savouries and quiches

Tesco chicken spring rolls
Tesco prawn spring rolls
Tesco crispy bake pork pie
Tesco crispy bake buffet pork pies
Tesco crispy bake lattice pork pie
Tesco crispy bake pork and egg pie
Tesco roast chicken puff pie
Tesco farmhouse potato tomato/bacon/
   sausage slice
Tesco puff lamb in gravy pie
Tesco sausage rolls
Tesco individual/family quorn and mushroom
   pies (frozen)
Tesco sausage rolls (frozen)
Tesco cottage pie

Tesco deep-filled steak and ale pie
Tesco chicken and vegetable pie
Tesco steak and horseradish mash pie
Tesco mini assorted Chinese snacks
Safeway beef and mushroom pie (deep dish
    and ordinary)
Safeway steak and ale pie (deep dish and
    ordinary)
Safeway baked bean and cheese flan
Safeway cheese and tomato quiche
Safeway smoked bacon quiche
Safeway quiche lorraine
Safeway sausage rolls
Safeway Cornish pasty
M&S vegetable spring roll
Co-op vegetable spring rolls
Co-op beef and mushroom pie (deep dish and
    ordinary)
Co-op steak and ale pie (deep dish and
    ordinary)
Somerfield mini Melton Mowbray pork pies
Somerfield sausage rolls
Somerfield cheese and onion savoury slices
Somerfield chicken and mushroom savoury
    slices
Somerfield mince beef and onion savoury
    slices
Somerfield Cornish pasties

Somerfield cheese and onion pasties
Somerfield chicken and mushroom pies
Somerfield mince beef and onion pies
Somerfield steak and kidney pies
Somerfield vegetable spring rolls
Somerfield pork cocktail sausage rolls
Somerfield cottage pie
Somerfield crispy baked pork pie
Somerfield crispy baked suet crust pie, steak
    and kidney
Somerfield Cumberland pie
Somerfield deep-filled chicken, mushroom and
    bacon pie
Somerfield deep-filled steak and kidney pie
Somerfield homestyle cottage pie
Somerfield homestyle Cumberland pie
Somerfield mighty pie chicken and vegetable
Somerfield mighty pie mince beef and potato
Somerfield pub-style chicken mushroom and
    bacon pie
Somerfield pub-style steak and mushroom in
    ale pie
Somerfield sausage and bacon rolls
Somerfield roast chicken and vegetable
    shortcrust pie
Somerfield vegetable and cheese shortcrust
    pie
Somerfield tray-baked Cornish shortcrust pie

Somerfield tray-baked sausage and onion
   shortcrust pie
Somerfield salmon and asparagus lattice slice
Somerfield lattice slice, roast chicken and
   broccoli
Somerfield party size sausage rolls (frozen)

Prepared seafood-based products and meals

Tesco prawn spring rolls
Tesco prawns in ginger sauce and vegetables
Tesco salmon fishcakes
Tesco Louisiana style jambalaya
Tesco New England smoked haddock chowder
Tesco prawn toasts
Safeway fish shapes
Safeway fish bites
Safeway chunky cod fillets in crispy crumb
Safeway chunky cod fillets in crispy batter
Safeway cod portions in crispy crumb
Safeway haddock portions in crunchy crumb
Safeway haddock portions in crispy batter
Safeway invitations – cod fillet goujons
Co-op smoked salmon mousse
Somerfield cod toppers with peppers, garlic
   and parmesan
Somerfield tuna burgers
Somerfield breaded fish goujons

Somerfield breaded seafood selection
Somerfield salmon and asparagus lattice slice
Somerfield seafood steaks
Somerfield tuna nicoise

Prepared vegetable-based products and meals

Tesco spinach and ricotta cannelloni
Tesco vegetarian cottage pie (frozen)
Tesco meat free carrot and coriander slices
Tesco Chinese egg fried rice
Tesco Chinese special fried rice
Tesco vegetable chow mein
Tesco baked potato and ratatouille snack
  pot
Tesco linguine puttanesca
Tesco roasted vegetable lasagne
Tesco healthy eating vegetable tagliatelle
Tesco spicy potato bhaji
Tesco gobi aloo saag
Tesco pilau rice
Tesco vegetable masala rice bow
Sainsbury's couscous onion and bacon flavour
Sainsbury's soya mince
Sainsbury's soya chunks
Sainsbury's vegetable ravioli
Sainsbury's traditional-style vegetarian
  moussaka

Sainsbury's traditional-style vegetarian cottage pie

Sainsbury's bolognese-style soya mince

Sainsbury's Mexican chilli-style soya mince

Sainsbury's soya mince and onions

Sainsbury's curry-style soya mince

Safeway breaded baby sweetcorn (frozen)

Safeway breaded red pepper strips (frozen)

Safeway breaded garlic mushrooms (frozen)

Safeway potato fingers (frozen)

Safeway cheesy potato nuggets

Safeway battered onion rings

Safeway spicy potato wedges

Safeway ravioli in tomato sauce

Asda spicy vegetable burgers (frozen)

Asda Mexican selection pack (frozen)

M&S rice, spinach and mushroom-filled pancakes

M&S celeriac gratin

M&S parsnip gruyère bake

M&S low-fat cauliflower cheese

M&S Singapore noodles

M&S special fried rice

Co-op savoury rice – sweet-and-sour

Co-op savoury rice – mushroom flavour

Co-op savoury rice – curry flavour

Co-op savoury rice – mixed vegetables

Co-op vegetable slices

Co-op vegetable curry with rice
Co-op vegetable quarter-pounders
Co-op large pancakes
Co-op three-cheese ravioli
Somerfield cheese and bean enchiladas
Morrisons vegetarian burgers (three varieties)

Pâtés, savoury spreads and dips
Tesco luxury dips
Sainsbury's beef pâté
Sainsbury's chicken and ham pâté
Sainsbury's chicken pâté
Sainsbury's chilli bean pâté
Sainsbury's crab pâté
Sainsbury's pizza pâté
Sainsbury's salmon and shrimp pâté
Sainsbury's sardine and tomato pâté
Sainsbury's tuna and mayonnaise pâté
Sainsbury's vegetable pâté
Sainsbury's chicken spread
Sainsbury's crab spread
Sainsbury's salmon spread
Sainsbury's sardine and tomato spread
Asda crunchy peanut butter
Asda sandwich paste – ham and beef
Asda farm stores sandwich paste – salmon
Asda farm stores sandwich paste – chicken
M&S houmous

Somerfield basic ham and beef paste
Somerfield basic salmon paste
Somerfield cheese and ham nibbles

Sauces, dressings and mixes

Tesco brown sauce
Tesco noodle sauce green Thai curry
Tesco noodle sauce szechuan
Tesco black bean stir fry sauce
Tesco taste of orient Hoisin sauce
Tesco fresh carbonara pasta sauce
Tesco fresh vegetable pasta sauce
Tesco fresh mushroom and mascarpone pasta
  sauce
Tesco fresh cheese pasta sauce
Tesco quattro formaggio pasta sauce
Tesco fresh napoletana pasta sauce
Tesco fresh arrabiata pasta sauce
Tesco fresh korma sauce
Tesco fresh Madras sauce
Tesco healthy eating carbonara sauce
Tesco fresh noodle sweet and sour sauce
Tesco fresh noodle black bean sauce
Sainsbury's hoisin sauce
Sainsbury's ginger garlic and chilli sauce
Sainsbury's zesty orange sauce
Sainsbury's fruity blackcurrant sauce
Safeway fresh hollandaise sauce

Safeway slimmer cheese sauce mix
Safeway instant cheese sauce mix
Asda farm stores batter mix
Asda farm stores victoria sponge mix
Co-op thousand islands dressing
Co-op virtually fat-free dressing
Co-op garlic and herb dressing
Waitrose teriyaki sauce
Somerfield fresh creamy mushroom
   sauce
Somerfield fresh spicy tomato sauce
Somerfield basics brown sauce
Somerfield mayonnaise
Somerfield reduced-calorie mayonnaise
Morrisons hollandaise sauce
Morrisons parsley sauce
Morrisons pancake mix
Morrisons Yorkshire pudding mix

Sandwiches
Tesco chargrilled chicken and vegetable
Tesco chicken and stuffing
Safeway pork and stuffing
Safeway chicken triple
Safeway roast chicken and stuffing
Safeway all day breakfast
Safeway brunch triple (sausage)
Safeway chicken tikka

Safeway exotic chicken triple

Safeway ploughman's salad roll

Asda chicken tikka

Asda lemon chicken

M&S healthy choice chicken and salad
sandwiches

M&S healthy choice chicken selection:
tandoori/lime coriander/tikka

M&S healthy choice aromatic duck

Somerfield bacon, lettuce and tomato with
mayonnaise

Dairy foods, fats, oils, margarines and spreads

Tesco pure corn oil

Co-op cheeses (those described as suitable for
vegetarians)

Somerfield soya spread

Pizzas

Tesco classico capriciosia pizza

Safeway thin and crispy cheese and tomato
(frozen)

Safeway thin and crispy pepperoni (frozen)

Safeway ham and pineapple (frozen)

Safeway thin and crispy ham and mushroom
(frozen)

Safeway triple-decker ham and pineapple

Safeway triple-decker meat supreme
Somerfield deep and crispy brunch
Somerfield deep and crispy cheese and tomato
Somerfield deep and crispy ham and
  pineapple
Somerfield deep and crispy pepperoni
Somerfield deep and crispy vegetable

Crisps, nuts and other packet snacks

Tesco tortilla chips (range of flavours)
Tesco bacon rashers
Tesco ricos cool original corn chips
Tesco sweet-and-sour crackers
Tesco ricos tangy cheese corn chips
Tesco assorted snacks bag
Tesco cheese and ham party snacks
Safeway tortilla chips (various flavours)
Safeway salt and black pepper cashew nuts
M&S authentic tortilla chips
Somerfield ham and cheese nibbles
Somerfield snack mix

Soups

Tesco tomato soup
Tesco chicken soup
Tesco vegetable soup
Tesco brown lentil soup
Tesco fresh chunky minestrone soup

Asda farm stores tomato soup
Asda minestrone soup
Co-op vegetable and chicken chunky soup
Somerfield homestyle creamy mushroom soup
Somerfield homestyle Italian-style tomato soup
Somerfield leek and potato soup
Somerfield cream of chicken soup
Somerfield oxtail soup

Desserts, cakes, biscuits and sweet snacks

Tesco mallow mixed tub
Tesco milk chocolate sauce
Tesco dark chocolate sauce
Tesco banoffee pie
Tesco egg custard tart
Tesco custard tart
Tesco fresh raspberry and cream victoria sandwich
Tesco dairy cream blueberry muffin
Tesco dairy cream meringues
Tesco dairy cream horns
Tesco dairy cream eclairs
Tesco custard doughnuts
Tesco chocolate eclairs
Tesco happy birthday present cake
Tesco happy birthday rose cake
Tesco truly fruity barm brack

Tesco mini chocolate chip cookies
Tesco 25% less fat rich tea biscuits
Tesco finest Belgian chocolate almond thins
Safeway ice-cream roll
Safeway lemon meringue pie (in the coffee
    shop)
Safeway savers dairy cream sponge
Safeway collectables chocolate spread
Safeway collectables chocolate and vanilla
    spread
Asda fresh cream vanilla sponge
Asda four-packet donut and eclair
Asda premium chocolate sponge
Asda premium vanilla sponge
Asda mini Danish selection
Asda apple donut
Asda mini sponge in four-pack assortment
Asda twin-pack cream scone
Asda shortbread fingers
Co-op luxury iced fruit bar
Co-op trifle range
Co-op toffee-coated popcorn
Co-op nice biscuits
Co-op cherry Genoa cake
M&S 95% fat-free clotted-cream rice
    pudding
Somerfield basics Madeira cake
Somerfield iced-top fruit bar

Somerfield luxury iced-top fruit bar
Somerfield mulled wine cake
Somerfield mini chocolate sponge puddings
Somerfield sticky toffee sponge puddings
Somerfield mini syrup sponge puddings
Somerfield carrot sponge pudding
Somerfield chocolate sponge pudding
Somerfield basics twelve milk chocolate coated
   twin wafer biscuits
Somerfield snack mix
Somerfield American-style snack mix

Miscellaneous
Sainsbury's tomato purée
Safeway double concentrated tomato purée

Part 5

How to avoid GM foods when you eat out

What restaurants have to tell you about GM food

The Government has told restaurants that they have to label GM foods. It says this will give diners the choice of whether or not they eat them. However, despite the grandiose claims made for the effectiveness of this approach, the labelling laws now in force for restaurants are still likely to leave everyone – staff and diners – thoroughly confused.

Most foods don't have to be labelled

The labelling regulations for restaurants, just like those for food retailers, apply only to the few foods with detectable levels of protein or DNA from a GM crop.

They do not cover the majority of foods that contain derivatives of GM crops (such as tomato purée) or products that are made using GM processing aids (such as vegetarian cheese made using chymosin, the GM rennet substitute).

How the few foods must be labelled

Foods with GM ingredients that need to be labelled by law do not have to be picked out individually on the menu. Restaurants can just put a general notice on their menu to the effect that diners only need to ask staff if they want to find out whether a dish has a GM ingredient.

Because the restaurant labelling regulations were put into immediate effect in March 1999 without any forewarning, the restaurant trade had no opportunity to train its staff. Table staff in most restaurants are therefore likely to be as deeply confused about what ingredients are GM or non-GM as any other member of the population.

Voluntary declarations and labels

In an attempt to clarify matters, many independent restaurants are likely to state their policy towards GM food on their menus in the form of 'GM-free zone'-type declarations. While these provide an interesting insight into a particular restaurant's stance, they are not independently audited and therefore not reliable. Most chain restaurants have developed a corporate policy covering all of their outlets and will state this on their menus. (See 'Where the fast-food chains stand'.)

Where the fast-food chains stand

This section outlines the policies of the biggest fast-food restaurant chains and outlets with a sizeable lunch-time take-away trade. You can use it to give your business to chains with a robust anti-GM food stand. Companies are given one of three ratings:*

Green Companies who have eliminated GM ingredients.

Amber Companies who are considering eliminating GM ingredients or who want to be GM free.

Red Companies who are not seeking to eliminate GM ingredients in their food.

* Ratings based on information supplied by company but not independently audited.

Green chains
Burger King
Domino Pizza
Holland and Barrett
Kentucky Fried Chicken
McDonald's
Perfect Pizza
Pizza Express

Amber chains
Caffé Uno
Deep Pan Pizza
Prêt à Manger
Wimpy

Red chains
Bella Pasta
Boots the Chemist
Pizza Hut

Part 6

Other action
you can take

Ways to influence supermarkets

Supermarkets are extremely sensitive to consumer action. Use the section 'Where the supermarkets stand on GM foods' to see what position your supermarket has adopted. So far, Iceland is the only UK chain to adopt an unequivocal position against GM food, but others, such as Asda and the Co-op, are expressing reservations. The chains originally most in favour of GM food are now playing down their commitment to it. All chains are actively trying to reformulate products so that their use of GM ingredients can be minimised.

By putting pressure on your supermarket to adopt an anti-GM food stand, you can send them the message that if they want to keep their customers happy, GM food is a commercial disaster. In the current climate, this sort of direct pressure can be extremely effective in getting supermarkets to rethink policy.

Write a letter
Comments delivered by phone, and notes scribbled in customer suggestions books, are notorious for disappearing into a big, black supermarket hole. However, supermarkets take well-considered letters quite seriously. They

have to be answered by a named representative of the supermarket and get logged at head office.

Letters that raise specific questions, for example, 'What independent tests has your chain carried out into the possible adverse effects of GM food on human health?' or 'How can you be sure that your conventional soya supplies are not being contaminated with GM supplies?', are harder to palm off with a bland response. So these will often have to be answered by technical staff in the company. This helps spread the idea around these chains that GM foods are more bother than they are worth.

Don't mess around writing to the manager of your local store, though. Go straight for head office and mark your letter for the attention of the Chief Executive. You can get the name by calling the numbers listed below.

In a letter you can explain

- Why you are opposed to GM foods (see Part One for a summary of the arguments)

- That you want the chain to boycott GM foods

- That Iceland in the UK and Carrefour,

France's biggest hypermarket chain, has done this already so such a move is perfectly feasible

- That you intend to shop elsewhere if it doesn't.

Send back your 'loyalty' card

When you get a typical 'reassuring' but unsatisfactory response to a letter, don't be surprised. You will have put pressure on the company even if it shows no signs of really taking on board your demand. If you still want to go further, return any loyalty or reward card for the chain that you might have along with a letter saying that if it continues to stock GM food, it does not deserve your loyalty. You can add that you intend to give your business to competitors with more robust anti-GM food policies.

Ask for a list

If you have become too attached to your loyalty card to make the above gesture, you can still demand a list of genetically modified foods, saying that you will use it to avoid them. Some, but not all, chains have started giving out lists of GM products that they are obliged by law to label. You will probably only get a very limited list, which is unlikely to cover any 'derivatives' of GM crops. But even asking for this helps keep up the pressure and acts as a reminder to head office that the GM issue won't go away.

Asda

Asda House
South Bank
Great Wilson Street
Leeds
Tel: 0500 100 055 (freephone)
http://www.asda.co.uk

Co-op (CWS)

Freepost MR 9473
Manchester M4 8BA
Tel: 0800 317 827
http://www.co-op.co.uk

Iceland

Second Avenue
Deeside Industrial Park
Deeside Flintshire
CH5 2NW
Tel: 0990 133 373 – hotline for info packs only
Tel: 01244 842 675 – general line for specific enquiries
http://www.iceland.co.uk

Marks & Spencer

Michael House
47 Baker Street
London
W1A 1DN
Tel: 0800 389 4367 (GM hotline – freephone)
http://marksandspencer.co.uk

Wm Morrison

Customer Service
Junction 41 Industrial Estate
Wakefield
WF2 OXF
Tel: 01924 870 000
www.morrisons.plc.uk

Sainsbury's

Stamford House
Stamford Street
London
SE1 9LL
Tel: 0800 636 262 (freephone)
http://www.sainsbury's.co.uk

Safeway
6 Millington Road
Hayes
Middlesex
UB3 4AY
Tel: 01622 712 987
http://www.safeway.co.uk

Somerfield/ Kwiksave/ Gateway
Somerfield House
Whitchurch Lane
Bristol
BS14 OTJ
Tel: 0117 939 9359
http://www.somerfield.co.uk

Tesco
Tesco House
PO Box 18
Delamere Road
Cheshunt
Hertfordshire
EN8 9SL
Tel: 0800 505 555 (freephone)
http://www.tesco.co.uk

Waitrose
Doncastle Road
Bracknell
Berkshire
RG12 8YA
Tel: 0800 188 884
http://www.waitrose.co.uk

Ways to influence politicians and regulators

Until recently, GM food was a consumer issue that bubbled away behind the scenes but never really made it into the formal political arena. Now intense public opposition to GM food in the UK has kicked it right up that political agenda.

Tony Blair and the Labour Party

Tony Blair has nailed his colours to the mast as a staunch defender of GM foods. He has tried to dismiss the overwhelming public opposition as a media-fanned food scare and fallen back on now-familiar assurances that the public should trust government scientists and regulators to protect public health and the environment.

You can write to him, pointing out that he is acting in a deeply undemocratic way – poll after poll shows that between 70 and 90 per cent of consumers do not want to eat GM food. You can say that his position is a vote-loser for the Labour Party.

If you are a member of the Labour Party, you can consider resigning over this fundamental issue and return your membership card to him directly explaining why.

If you are a Labour voter, you can tell him that you are considering voting in forthcoming elections for another party with an anti-GM food stance.

The Conservative and other opposition parties

The Conservatives support a five-year moratorium on GM crops, as do the Lib Dems. The Scottish National Party supports a moratorium on the planting of GM crops. The Green Party is a long-standing opponent of GM food and crops.

You can write to the leaders of these parties applauding their action to date and asking them to keep up the pressure.

Local politicians

Many local authorities throughout the UK have already declared that they wish to ban GM food in school meals and other local-authority establishments. They have asked their catering services to set about eliminating GM ingredients from the food they provide. This is an almost impossible task, because this type of low- cost, institutional catering relies precisely on the sort of heavily processed food – burgers, sausages and so on – that is most likely to contain invisible (unlabelled) GM ingredients. So it is very difficult for caterers to find out which foods could be affected.

However, although the practicality of implementing a ban is debatable, by adopting an anti-GM position, local authorities put political pressure on government to listen to what consumers are saying on the issue. So if your local authority has not yet adopted such a ban, you can lobby it to do so.

Your MEP

Many of the vital overall policy decisions concerning GM food are made at a European level. This is why the biotech companies have been so active behind the scenes there, trying to influence the regulatory framework set for GM foods by the European Commission. They have been successful to date in seeing that any regulation of GM food is weak. This is why, for example, very few foods with GM ingredients need to be labelled.

Your MEP is your elected representative to the European parliament and can instigate or support regulation which would give the biotech companies less room to manoeuvre and reflect the consumer consensus for a moratorium on GM foods and crops.

You can get in touch with your MEP, outline your concerns, and lobby him or her on the issue.

Part 7

Where to find out more about genetically modified food

Some of the groups opposed to genetic modification of food have little or no funding, so check if an SAE is required or if there is a nominal charge for more detailed briefings.

Freeze

94 White Lion Street
London N1 9PF
Tel: 0171 837 0642
Email: gealliance@dial.pipex.com

A wide coalition of individuals and organisations calling for a five-year freeze on GM food in order to assess all the implications for consumers, farmers and the environment. Send a fifty-pence SAE and you will get 'freeze' postcards to send to MPs and leaflets.

Friends of the Earth UK

26-28 Underwood Street
London N1 7JQ
Tel: 0171 490 1555
Email: Info@foe.co.uk
Web: http://www.foe.co.uk

Campaigning for a five-year freeze on GM foods and a switch to sustainable farming. Free briefings and leaflets available.

GenEthics News

PO Box 6313
London N16 ODY
Tel: 0181 809 4513
Email: genethicsnews@compuserve.com
Web: http://www.ourworld.compuserve.com

Publishes a bimonthly newsletter on the ethical, social and environmental issues raised by genetic engineering.

Genetics Concern

14 Upper Pembroke Street
Dublin 2
Tel:++ 353 1 6618 123
Email: geneticsconcern@tinet.ie

Raises awareness about the potential dangers of GM food and agriculture. It has a newsletter for members and a free email service, 'Genetwork'.

Genetic Engineering Network (GEN)

PO Box 9656
London N4 4JY
Tel: 0181 374 9516
Email: genetics@gn.apc.org
Web: http://www.genetix.org

Supports anti-GM food groups by providing information. Produces a bimonthly newsletter 'genetix update' and runs email information lists.

Genetics Forum

94 White Lion Street
London N1 9PF
Tel: 0171 837 9229
Email: geneticforum@gn.apc.org
Web: http://www.geneticsforum.org.uk

Publishes *Splice* magazine, which investigates biotechnology issues and reports on GM food developments.

Genetix Food Alert

23 Fleming Street
Glasgow G31 1PQ
Tel: 0141 554 6099
Email: lindsay@gntx.freeserve.co.uk
Web: http://www.essential-trading.co.uk/genetix.htm

Coalition of GM-free wholefood trade.

Genewatch

The Courtyard
Whitecross Road
Tideswell
Buxton
Derbyshire SK17 8NY
Tel: 01298 871898
Email: gene.watch@dial.pipex.com
Web: http://www.genewatch.org

Monitors GM food developments and produces regular briefings.

Green Party

1a Waterlow Road
London N19 5NJ
Tel: 0171 272 4474
Email: office@greenparty.org.uk
Web: http://www.greenparty.org.uk

Campaigns for GM-free school meals. For general pack on GM issues, call 01484 430 738.

Greenpeace UK

Canonbury Villas
Islington
London N1 2PN
Tel: 0171 865 8100
True Food Hotline (GM food) 0171 865 8222
Email: info@uk.greenpeace.org
Web: http://www.greenpeace.org/truefood

Campaigns for a global ban on GM food and
for organic food. Has 'True Food' campaign
and other leaflets.

HRH Prince Charles, Prince of Wales

Web: http://www.princeofwales.gov.uk/forum

Prince Charles is opposed to genetic modification of food and has set up a web site to
stimulate public debate on GM issues.

Monsanto

PO Box 53
High Wycombe HP12 4HL
Tel: 01494 474 918

The biotech company that brought us GM soya.
Represents the pro-GM lobby. Extensive web
site, mailing list and other information.

Soil Association

Bristol House
40-56 Victoria Street
Bristol BS1 6BY
Tel: 01179 142 449
Email: info@soilassociation.org
Web: http://www.soilassociation.org

Campaigning for organic food and to ban genetic modification in food and farming. Has a free GM information pack and 'what you can do' sheets. Publishes 'Where to Buy Organic Food', a directory by region of farm shops, box schemes and retailers, £5.00 including postage and packing.

WEN (Women's Environmental Network)

Test Tube Harvest Campaign
97 Worship Street
London EC2A 2BE
Tel: 0171 247 3327
Email: TestTube@gn.apc.org

Campaigns for a freeze on GM food and agriculture. Briefings, campaign pack and leaflets available.

Women's Nutritional Advisory Service

PO Box 268
Lewes
East Sussex BN7 2QN
Tel: 01273 487 3666
Email:wnas@wnas.org.uk
Web: http://www.wnas.org.uk

Has conducted a survey of companies on whether they use GM soya. List available with an SAE.

THE FOOD OUR CHILDREN EAT
Joanna Blythman

Leading investigative food journalist Joanna
Blythman examines the decline in standard of
the food our children eat and provides useful
strategies on how to avoid dinner-time disasters.

£8.99   1 85702 936 4

THE SHOPPER'S GUIDE TO
ORGANIC FOOD
Lynda Brown

Journalist and broadcaster Lynda Brown cuts
through the red tape to reveal the best ways to
buy organic food.

£7.99   1 85702 840 6

HOW TO ORDER

**All Fourth Estate books are available from your local bookshop, or can
be ordered direct (FREE UK p&p) from:**

Fourth Estate, Book Service By Post, PO Box 29,
Douglas, I-O-M, IM99 1BQ   *Credit cards accepted.*
Tel: 01624 836000   Fax: 01624 670923
Internet: http://www.bookpost.co.uk   e-mail: bookshop@enterprise.net

*All prices are correct at time of going to press, but may be subject to change.
Please state when ordering if you do **not** wish to receive further information
about Fourth Estate titles.*